In the Hurricane's Wake

In the Hurricane's Wake

David Alan Hoag

Library of Congress Control Number:		2019918053
ISBN:	Hardcover	978-1-7960-6992-1
	Softcover	978-1-7960-6991-4
	eBook	978-1-7960-6990-7

To order additional copies of this book, contact:
Xlibris
1-888-795-4274
www.Xlibris.com
Orders@Xlibris.com
805158

CONTENTS

Introduction..xi

Acknowledgements...xiii

1 Humor and Encouragement 1

    1.1 Management 101 2

    1.2 Terah's Finals..3

    1.3 Close Shave...4

    1.4 Bridge Support...5

    1.5 Creative Yanamation...6

    1.6 Time Dilation Task 8

    1.7 St. Paddy's Day with Velinda......................................9

    1.8 Can You Hear Me Now?...10

    1.9 Aim High 12

    1.10 Circadian Rhythm Sanity Check for Couples 13

    1.11 Communicator Confusion 14

    1.12 Communicator Colors 15

    1.13 The Trench 16

    1.14 Time...17

    1.15 Yana's Road Not Taken...18

    1.16 Legacy..20

    1.17 Door Repair Request 21

    1.18 Fitness for Duty 22

    1.19 Unfit Bit...23

    1.20 Get with the Program 24

    1.21 In Honor of Monica Martin's Cat Returning Home.........25

    1.22 Ties That Binder 26

    1.23 Greg Eyvazian's Lament...28

    1.24 Yoda's Take on Proposals...29

    1.25 If Only...30

    1.26 Doc Martin's B-Day...31

    1.27 Basis of Fact..32

1.28 Pirate's Lament 34
1.29 Softball Game Tonight 35
1.30 Forgiving Heart 36

2 Epic Poems 37

2.1 Gorm Grymme 38
2.2 Accidental Causes 41
2.3 The Art of a Muse 44

3 Iambic Pentameter 55

3.1 Glimmering Hope 56
3.2 Fourth of July 57
3.3 For Glory 58

4 Limericks 59

4.1 On Vacation 61
4.2 Diversity 62
4.3 Adam's Birthday 63
4.4 Shower Challenge 64
4.5 Treasure 65
4.6 Nick's Birthday 66
4.7 Limerick for David Lappa 67
4.8 Read and Sign 68
4.9 Scouting the Territory 69
4.10 A Limerick for Gary Wilkinson 70
4.11 SNAFU 72
4.12 A Limerick for Mark Lehman 73
4.13 A Limerick for Omed Muzaffrey 74
4.14 Omed Moved 75
4.15 For Allen Barker 76
4.16 Currency of the Dead 77
4.17 FBC Pickers 78
4.18 What Prize? 79
4.19 Muscovy Duck 80
4.20 Twister 81
4.21 Time Off 82
4.22 Beans? Again? 83
4.23 Failure Modes and Effects Analysis 84
4.24 Limerick Power 85
4.25 Stuntman 86

5 Commemorative Poems...87

   5.1 Lunar Dreams...88

   5.2 In the Hurricane's Wake................................. 90

   5.3 A Father's Questions..91

   5.4 The Real Diehl...92

   5.5 Send-off...93

   5.6 Citizen Soldier..94

   5.7 The Clueless Father of Daughters....................96

   5.8 Thanksgiving Reflections................................98

   5.9 Magic...99

   5.10 Knocking 100

   5.11 It Seemed So Easy 102

   5.12 Brush Strokes..104

   5.13 Glitter and Glue..106

   5.14 To My Lover..107

   5.15 Hard Rock Valentine 108

   5.16 William and Kate 110

   5.17 Unseen Power..111

   5.18 American Life: Power...................................112

   5.19 A Line for Dad's Seventieth.........................114

   5.20 Stopping by Triconex on a Rainy Evening 115

   5.21 Santa Ana Winds 116

   5.22 Be My Valentine..117

   5.23 Witnessed by Clowns 118

   5.24 Finger on the Pulse......................................121

   5.25 Lake Forest Apiary 122

6 In Memoriam 123

   6.1 Michael Hoag - In Memoriam.......................124

   6.2 True Quality...126

   6.3 The Reminder 127

   6.4 Eulogy...128

   6.5 With a Whimper...129

   6.6 Me Grandma..130

   6.7 Phoenix Rises 132

   6.8 On My Mother's Passing................................134

   6.9 The Crossing 136

   6.10 Waving Goodbye...138

   6.11 Eternity...140

   6.12 Requiem..141

7 Songs 143

   7.1 I Am So Frozen 145
   7.2 Both Sides Now 146
   7.3 New Sesame Street Theme Lyrics 148
   7.4 Did You Know Recovery's in Sight? 149
   7.5 Softball at Trabuco High 150
   7.6 Term! Term! Term! 151
   7.7 Navy Training Chant 152
   7.8 I Get a Kick From I/O 153
   7.9 Friday Friday 154
   7.10 Performer's Prayer 156
   7.11 The Island's Untold Tale 158
   7.12 Chicken Attack 160
   7.13 The Class Theme Song 162
   7.14 I'd Better Settle Down 164
   7.15 The Sound of Sniffles 166
   7.16 B. I. C. – Boyz In Confirmation 168
   7.17 The Sounds of Safety 170
   7.18 It's Scott and Dan 172
   7.19 I'm Off to Take a Journey 174
   7.20 Dust in the Bag 175

8 Odes 177

   8.1 Ode to the PM's Delivery 178
   8.2 Growing Up Too Fast 179
   8.3 Extinction 180
   8.4 Ode ad Draconis Infinitas 182
   8.5 Yana Reznik's Lost Performance 183
   8.6 Satisfying the Ghost 184
   8.7 Ever Changing Profile 185
   8.8 On a Creative Note 186
   8.9 Love One Another 188
   8.10 Joaquin's 190

9 Christmas Cards 191

   9.1 2015 Christmas Card - A Savior Has Been Born to You ... 193
   9.2 2016 Christmas Card - Welcome to the Family 194
   9.3 2017 Christmas Card - Angels Rejoiced 196
   9.4 2018 Christmas Card - A Christmas Message 198
   9.5 2019 Christmas Card – A Christmas Wish 200

10 Geocaching Related...203

    10.1 Cigam Finds The Da Vinci Codes - Part 1.....................204
    10.2 Cigam Finds The Da Vinci Codes - Part 2 205
    10.3 Cigam Finds The Da Vinci Codes - Part 3 206
    10.4 Cigam Finds The Da Vinci Codes - Part 4......................207
    10.5 Cigam Casts a Hex 208
    10.6 Cigam Rides Again 209
    10.7 A Bird in the Hand..210

11 RuneScape Related 211

    11.1 Party Hat 213
    11.2 The Sith Order 214
    11.3 Wishing for Relief 216
    11.4 Cannonballs 217
    11.5 Dragons 218
    11.6 Terah..219
    11.7 Member Bonus...220
    11.8 Of Cabbages and Kings......................................221
    11.9 Drawn...222
    11.10 MCM Entry...223
    11.11 Lumbridge...224
    11.12 King Black Dragon 226
    11.13 They Spawn Anew Each Wednesday Morn...................228
    11.14 My Avatar Gently Weeps....................................230

12 Puzzle Solutions 231

    12.1 Explanation: Cigam Finds The Da Vinci Codes - Part 1....232
    12.2 Explanation: Cigam Finds The Da Vinci Codes - Part 2....234
    12.3 Explanation: Cigam Finds The Da Vinci Codes - Part 3....236
    12.4 Explanation: Cigam Finds The Da Vinci Codes - Part 4....238
    12.5 Explanation: Cigam Casts a Hex 240

13 Final Thoughts 243

INTRODUCTION

A while ago, a good friend of mine asked me who I felt had influenced my poetic/literary life. It's not often that I contemplate who my poetic/literary influences are; it's even less often that I'm asked who they might be. The consideration of that question, and the answers actually turned out to be an interesting exploration.

I would have to say that one of the earliest poetic/literary influences in my life would have to be the good Dr. Seuss. Theodor Seuss Geisel produced such an amazing body of work, won so many literary awards, and has imparted some wonderful philosophy into the minds of millions of children… and even a few adults. He elevated the cadence and rhyme of traditional poetry to fine art, while keeping it grounded in the imagination of childhood. Two of the earliest books I remember reading on my own (over and over) were *And to Think That I Saw It on Mulberry Street* and *McElligot's Pool*, books that spurred my young imagination to soar. His works have stayed fresh in my mind, as I have read them aloud to a generation of my own children, and now to a new generation of grandchildren. I often quote from his writing, things like:

- "You have brains in your head. You have feet in your shoes. You can steer yourself any direction you choose."
- "Be who you are and say what you feel, because those who mind don't matter and those who matter don't mind."

Of course, as I matured from childhood, there were many other poetic/literary influences in my life: Asimov, Heinlein, Tolkien, Shakespeare, Dickens,

Twain, Poe, Steinbeck, Orwell, C.S. Lewis, Dante Alighieri, H.G. Wells, Jules Verne, and so many others. There is no doubt that I love to read, and that my taste in poetry and literature is very eclectic. Immersed in their works, there is no question that I would surface dripping with their influence.

And finally, there are a few poetic/literary influences in my life that have occurred at a deeper, more subliminal level. These were patterned onto my subconscious as I was read to, or otherwise absorbed their works in school or church. These are perhaps not my sought-out influences, but they are important, nonetheless. They would be authors like: Hans Christian Anderson, Rudyard Kipling, Lewis Carroll, Roald Dahl, Benjamin Franklin, Thomas Jefferson, Thomas Paine, and the various writers of the Bible. I'm often surprised by the poetry, knowledge, and insight of writers of the various books of the Bible. That what they wrote, thousands of years ago, still has any meaning is amazing. That it is directly applicable to the human condition, still today, seems nothing short of miraculous… or perhaps… God inspired.

> "For now, we see through a glass, darkly; but then face to face: now I know in part; but then shall I know even as also I am known." - 1 Corinthians 13:12 (KJV)

Now you know what has influenced me. What inspires me to write, though, is something quite different altogether. Inspiration can come as a word, a phrase, a song, an image, a person, or just a fleeting thought. Throughout this book, I have added notes [within square brackets] that may deliver some insight as to my original inspiration, background explanation, and perhaps a little backstory. Of course, over time, and given each individual reader's personal situation, MY inspiration may be of little or no consequence. If you find that to be the case, you can probably safely ignore anything I've included in square brackets.

If you experience half the enjoyment reading my poetry as I experienced while writing it, you're certain to have a good time within the pages of this book.

David Alan Hoag

᪶

Acknowledgements

My wife, Patti, is one of the world's best proofreaders and editors. Her keen editor's eye, emotional perception, and steady moral compass helped drive me to always push past "good enough."

Far back, in Greek mythology, there are nine sister goddesses called Muses who preside over and inspire art, science, song, and poetry. Today, a muse is defined as inspiration, creative influence, or stimulus. For me, there are companies, situations, co-workers, friends, and family that often act as that inspirational muse. In the notes associated with each poem I will often acknowledge my inspiration, sometimes even naming a particular muse.

As important as inspiration, however, is encouragement. Over the years, I have received a huge amount of encouragement from so many people that I cannot even begin to thank and recognize everyone. I hope that this book of my poetry encourages you in some way.

1 HUMOR AND ENCOURAGEMENT

Most of the poems in this section use humor to somehow encourage and lift people up in the midst of something I knew they were going through at the time. You will find no single poetic style in this section.

1.1 Management 101

by David Alan Hoag - April 12, 2013

So, you want to be a manager?
I'd advise you: "Pray, think twice!"
For, to be a first-rate manager
You must amputate your "nice."

Your advice may only just confuse
And your tasks must be all wet,
Your conflicting orders must insult
Like some petty martinet.

On second thought, here I must confess
You're impossible to train.
You'll NEVER be a manager, as
You have MORE than half a brain!

∼

[I sent this to a co-worker, to give her a laugh and some encouragement at a time when she was feeling pressured by her boss.]

1.2 Terah's Finals

by David Alan Hoag - April 29, 2013

Oh, ignominies this week
Include more finals testing.
With perceived need for cramming,
There's been no time for resting.

They really ought to measure
Teacher effectivity.
Ironically, to do that
They'll test recall skills by me.

Other students quake in fear,
But you see, I'm unafraid.
Whatever might transpire,
On a curve... I know they'll grade.

[Terah Blair, a good friend from the RuneScape realm, was stressing a little about an upcoming final exam, so I dashed off this poem to cheer her up.]

1.3 Close Shave

by David Alan Hoag - May 2, 2013

Every day, it seems to me,
I feel the swarm begin.
They crowd upon my cheekbones
And surge down from my chin.

And should I cut their numbers
In a scrappy, bloody fight,
I know they'll just come crawling back,
Ere dawn's first gleaming light.

Even when I think they're gone,
I know they're growing there.
Darkly, in the glass I see…
It's only facial hair.

❧

[This one was just for fun. As you might expect, inspiration hit early in the morning.]

1.4 Bridge Support

by David Alan Hoag - May 16, 2013

Yes, bridges may break,
At terrible cost
And it's hard to know
Just how they were lost.

Some fell due to storms.
Some... overly strained,
Most that went wanting
Were poorly maintained.

That oxidation?
Just flakey brown crust?
Never was treated,
So now it is rust.

Rust might be hidden,
Or gaping big hole;
Bridges, or people...
Rust weakens their soul.

Who are your bridges?
You care for them much?
Maintenance is simple,
With prayers and a touch.

Don't forget your span,
For you're a bridge, too.
You don't stand alone
I'm praying for you.

❧

[Inspired by Miranda Scales' heartfelt poem, "Bridges".]

1.5 Creative Yanamation

by David Alan Hoag - June 20, 2013

How does it feel to be a Muse?
And so creatively infuse
Into artistic heart and mind?
Inspiring works of every kind.

We share a little time with you
And suddenly, the world seems new
With vibrant and creative rush
You guide our camera, pen, and brush.

You are the joy to everyone:
To dreary thoughts, you bring the sun,
And when you're freed from house and room
You cause green fields to rise in bloom!

We, through our art, your praises sing
And thank you… for the YOU… you bring.

✺

[The painting *At Breakfast* inspired this poem… along with several pictures from Yana Reznik's latest trip to Russia, and the fact that it was Yana's birthday. As you might have guessed, the painting is of Yana. You can find photographs of Yana elsewhere in this book, as she has sparked many creative poetic excursions.]

1.6 Time Dilation Task

by David Alan Hoag - May 30, 2013

Expanding out
And spreading wide
The project task
And time divide.

And doing so
With super powers;
NOT expending
Project hours.

[This one was written for a project manager, to assure him that I was NOT charging any hours to his project.]

1.7 St. Paddy's Day with Velinda

by David Alan Hoag - March 17, 2014

I'll be by in a bit
Once me glass has been drained
And the toasts are all done
And the new barmaid's trained.

I'll be by in a bit
And I mean it, I'm sure
Sure, I'll be just a bit
On this Pub-Crawlin' tour.

I'll be by in a bit
But I can't find the door
Me judgment seems cloudy
So I'd best have one more.

HAPPY ST. PATRICK'S DAY

❧

[My thanks to co-worker and friend, Velinda Meza… the muse, and inspiration for this poem. Hmmm, I better make it clear that the inspiration Velinda supplied was only to message me to drop by her office. I said: "I'll be by in a bit." That, and the fact it was St. Patrick's Day, was the inspiration for the poem. Let imagination take flight!]

1.8 Can You Hear Me Now?

by David Alan Hoag - November 12, 2014

It's so hard to be an artist.
I suffer for my art.
My fingers pound the keys, till raw,
To give the world my heart.

I practice six or seven hours,
But only during days.
I might have played at 2 am,
But that's a drunken haze.

Now some neighbor's in an uproar;
He says he's bringing suit,
For my classical piano
Mutes X-men as they shoot.

So I'll practice my piano
Until the lawsuit comes.
And after that, I'll have you know,
I'm taking up the drums.

ès

[My friend and muse, Yana Reznik, is a professional pianist. During a time when she was living in an apartment in Chicago, she found an anonymous note stuck to her door. The note read:

"We all appreciate your passion for the piano, but this is out of control. There are days you play 6-7+ hours at a time, time you play at 2 am! You play during evening hours people are coming home to relax. You have a legit piano - do you realize how <u>LOUD</u> it is! Over surround sound to X-men movies 3 apartments away! For the love of God please find a way to keep it down, we're all sick of it."

I found it deliciously ironic that the anonymous neighbor complained that the piano was drowning out their surround sound of X-men movies. Surround sound often shakes the walls, floors, and ceilings of neighboring apartments. This neighbor likely thought nothing of the over -the-top volume of the continuous fighting, explosions, and destruction emanating from their X-men movies… only that Rachmaninov, Mozart, and Beethoven were somehow intruding on their enjoyment of classic movies.

You'll find a picture of the anonymous note, below.]

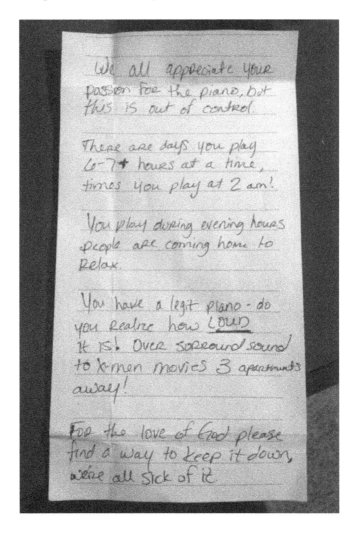

1.9 Aim High

By David Alan Hoag - September 12, 2002

At every turn, most every day
We must decide; we choose a way.
I'd look down in the noonday sun
At dusty paths, then start down one.

My way was dark, one lonely night
And all the paths: beyond my sight.
A voice, too small to comprehend,
Said: "Raise your sights, look up, my friend."

A star shone brightly in the sky
More than the rest, it caught my eye.
Though hard to see by light of day,
I chose the star as my new way.

There, high above my outstretched hand,
It pulled me on, across the land.
And were the oceans blocking me,
It kept me true, while on the sea.

The path that stretched so high for me
I followed with technology.
While others stop… and change abhor
Someday… I will… my star explore!

At every turn, most every day
YOU… must decide; YOU choose a way.
Perhaps, you'd wish to soar and fly,
Remember then, these words: "Aim High!"

꽁

1.10 Circadian Rhythm Sanity Check for Couples

by David Alan Hoag - September 1, 2013

Out of sync and out of phase
I like nights and you like days.
I'm always hot, you're always cold.
You're kind of shy, while I'm so bold.

Nature girl, you plant and sow;
I love plants… when they don't grow.
I'm fine that gardening is for you,
But why demand I garden, too?

If you're odd, it's just a quirk,
Odd in me, makes me a jerk.
You always make the best of time.
But my pursuits… are less sublime.

Our Circadian Measure
Causes you great displeasure.
Be warned! And I offer this fact:
Opposites… don't always attract!

❧

1.11 Communicator Confusion

by David Alan Hoag - April 11, 2013

Your light is green, but no response,
So I'm in the wind... Just flappin'.
You're either gone; your light's a lie,
Or I suspect... You're nappin'!

[Prompted by the failure of the Communicator office communication tool to connect me to Velinda Meza.]

1.12 Communicator Colors

by David Alan Hoag - May 11, 2012

Green, I'm in.
Salmon, I'm not.
Yellow, I'll be right back.
Red is a sign,
To go away.
I'm dead, if you see BLACK!

❧

[This described my "normal" status display on the Communicator office communication tool. Being ever the optimist, BLACK was not a viable option available to the tool.]

1.13 The Trench

by David Alan Hoag - Feb. 21, 2012

"I'd like to know about a trench,"
I queried learned men.
"Come take a look at all my maps,"
A geographer said, then.

"Geology is what you want;
See details of Earth's crust."
"Ah, but to map this ocean trench,
Geography's a must!"

"My learned friends, I interrupt,
Please do not try so hard
To paint each Study as the best.
The trench... it's in my yard."

❧

[This poem was inspired by Catarina Hernandez telling her sister, Cassandra Hernandez, about her college geology course and her professor explaining about an ocean trench; first posted on Facebook.]

1.14 Time

By David Alan Hoag - May 14, 2012

Time... an illusion;
A fast flowing flood,
A river of options sublime.
Eddies may hold you;
A slow, whirling grip.
What's a drop in the ocean of time?

You stand on the shore
A timesheet in hand
Marking time as it flows over me
You might track the tide,
But never the drops;
In the end, naught but futility.

~ॐ

[This poem was a humorous response to some urgent demand that I fill
out yet another timesheet... in an endless ocean of timesheets.]

1.15 Yana's Road Not Taken

by David Alan Hoag - August 4, 2015

Frost wrote of where two roads diverged,
And later telling with a sigh
Somewhere ages and ages hence:
He took the one less traveled by.

Musician, dancer, artisan
It seemed in art we chose to say:
"Secure and normal's not for us,
So let us take a different way."

There's certainly the Siren song
Of elusive fate's allure
That crumbles in the grueling light
Of performance, show, or tour.

Oh, heartbroken, we sometimes yearn
For a normal, average day
But artistic choices lead us on
Creative way upon new way.

Frost chose the road less traveled
In that yellow, wooded glade.
Like him, the road we've chosen,
All the difference it has made!

✺

[This poem took its inspiration from two sources. Obviously, Robert Frost was one, the other was a Facebook post by Yana Resnik on 8/4/15, which read:

"Heartbroken, tired, confused and uninspired. Yes, FB almost always sees the "happy days" and "happy posts" but all the struggle and challenges that any artist goes through are HELL on earth. Really! We see them on stage, beautiful, radiant, successful. We don't see the behind the scenes. In days like this I wonder why I haven't chosen an easier path, why I don't use my "other" talents, why can't I just have a "normal" life making steady money, having "normal" hours. Is it for the love of music? Stage? Applause? Creativity? Is it the struggle itself that is so masochistically attractive? Yes, all the above, but sometimes all you want is a little break. Or a miracle!!!"]

1.16 Legacy

David Alan Hoag - February 18, 2013

Leaving a legacy...
   to your children...
      to your team...
         to your community...

Is NOT about what you leave TO them,
   but what you leave IN them.

℞

1.17 Door Repair Request

by David Alan Hoag - August 14, 2015

We need repair; our door won't close,
Which seems a duplicate request.
The last solution that was tried
Has proven stop-gap, at its best.

Last hammered to a working state,
Again, this problem has arose.
The weakened plate (it's bent again)
Now thwarts the door's attempt to close.

The strike plate's bent, as you can see,
This violates security.
So, getting to the matter's heart,
I would suggest you change the part.

For me, I'd just replace the thing,
At least, that's what I know I'd do.
For now, I'll simply be content
To know it's in somebody's queue.

[After repeated attempts to get maintenance to fix the door to our supposedly secure area, I tried this poetic request. The part got replaced, and the door was repaired correctly, less than 24 hours later.]

1.18 Fitness for Duty

by David Alan Hoag - January 12, 2016

Before you submit to testing, remember:

If you want to get drunk
Or you want to get wired,
When they're testing your blood
You're "FIT" to be fired!

[This was part of a Fitness for Duty (FFD) chain of emails. Some industries require random testing for alcohol and/or drugs. The poem was just a spur-of-the-moment bit of humor to a friend about to undergo "Fitness for Duty" blood testing.]

1.19 Unfit Bit

by David Alan Hoag - March 3, 2016

Dave Hoag found my Fitbit
And he's such a nice guy,
But he doesn't move much.
Who knew Fitbits could die?!?

∾

[Carol Naus provided the impetus for this workplace poetry when she broadcast an email that described a Fitbit device that had been found. Of course, I didn't really find the missing Fitbit. These days, anything I see on the floor pretty much stays there.]

1.20 Get with the Program

by David Alan Hoag - May 5, 2014

```
FUNCTION VACATION_TIME
      IF Just-The-Facts THEN
```
I'll be taking a few vacation days over the Memorial Day weekend;

I'll be gone from Thursday (5/22) through Tuesday (5/27);

I'll be in Building 3, and back to work on Wednesday (5/28);

```
      ELSE
```
Memorial Day is on its way;
This year, the 26th of May,
And though it may be weeks away
I'm taking time, this holiday.

So without any more delay
I give you my communique,
With weeks of lead-time, by the way,
Re: pre-approved vacation pay.

May 22, I'm off to play
In cities near the Oakland bay,
But have no feelings of dismay
I'll soon return to Building "trey".

```
      END_IF;
END_FUNCTION;
```

∽

[I dashed this off as a notification that I was taking some vacation time. I wanted the poem to be in the format of a software program, hence the structure.]

1.21 In Honor of Monica Martin's Cat Returning Home

by David Alan Hoag - July 25, 2011

A hunter and sly promoter
Caught a mighty cat one day,
And just what kind of cat it was
The experts couldn't say.

So he went on tour; round-the-world,
And he charged a hefty fee.
"Come one, come all, to see the beast…
Just cough up some dough to me."

Scholars argued; most disagreed.
Some claimed it was Hawaiian.
But in the end, all did concur…
It has become fee-lion!

1.22 Ties That Binder

by David Alan Hoag - July 18, 2018

Hey, Framatome's moving
Though not very far.
On foot, not an hour,
Only minutes by car.

So now there's a scramble
To pack up and move
We've been told to condense
To help make it go smooth.

For extraneous paper,
Heed these reminders:
"Dump out files where you can
And empty your binders."

Well, the nuclear team's
An efficient crew
Fast emptying binders
By the hundreds! Who knew?!?

Binders on cabinets,
There's binders on chairs,
Binders in the hallways,
Binders clogging the stairs.

Binders breeding binders
That MUST be the case!
How else could the binders
Be all over the place?

Binders to the ceiling
Binders far and wider,
But we really don't care…
They're staying with Schneider!!!

[Our group was packing up in preparation for an impending move into new quarters. For a week, some unknown person had been leaving empty 3-ring binders atop file cabinets. This resulted in another "someone" emailing requests that the binders be removed. The upshot was that MORE binders appeared atop the file cabinets, inspiring the poem.]

1.23 Greg Eyvazian's Lament

by David Alan Hoag - April 26, 2018

Oh, I'll never play poker
With women or men;
I Won't play that game,
No, never again!

It's a con, rigged against me,
And wouldn't you know,
When I need the luck
The river won't flow.

Oh, this game is so evil,
This game is a sin,
Excepting, of course…
The times when I win!

1.24 Yoda's Take on Proposals

by David Alan Hoag - August 31, 2018

You may be disturbed,
Or offended, or hot,
But whatever your umbrage…
Surprised you are NOT!

[This poem was triggered by an email by one of the technical staff working on a project proposal that we had worked very hard to cut to the bone. Sales and management came back and demanded we cut yet another 5%… without them taking any cut. The staff member sent an email saying he was "disturbed".]

1.25 If Only

by David Alan Hoag - October 01, 2011

If only, if only,
The teenager said,
I could just get that Facebook out of my head
Still the task waits; books unopened and lonely
Just can't leave the web
If only, if only.

[Written for Michael Krauseman… at that time a teenager struggling to complete an assignment, all the while distracted by Facebook, messages, calls, and the World of Warcraft game.

The inspiration was from someone else singing the refrain from *If Only*, a song written by Andrew Davis, Louis Sachar, and Joel Clark McNeely, and performed by Fiction Plane.]

1.26 Doc Martin's B-Day

by David Alan Hoag - August 15, 2011

The learned Doctor Martin
Is so very, very clean
And though she's nice to circus folk,
Most Naugas think she's mean.

See... leather doesn't suit Marie
And it's well known far and wide:
She loves the feel of PVC,
Thus... she makes the Nauga hide!

[It was Marie Martin's birthday, so I offered up a poem I knew she'd like. Marie is an amazing human. She's a PhD, hails from an engineering and musical background, is a stilt walker, dancer, and circus performer. She may also secretly shelter several Naugas.]

1.27 Basis of Fact

by David Alan Hoag - November 02, 2018

A bass is a bass
But not always the case
'Cuz a bass is a bass
When you fish on your ass.

Then a base is a base
When you slide on your face
And it still is a base
as a headquarters place.

But a chemical base
might burn off your face
While the base I like best
Just supports all the rest.

And for all that it's worth
We are all based on Earth
So if puns are your taste
On them this poem is based.

Playing a bass.

1.28 Pirate's Lament

by David Alan Hoag – February 07, 2018

I've lost me gold earring;
Not a loss that I'd choose.
For a pirate, his earring
Is a heartbreak to lose.

Just a simple gold hoop
Of incalculable cost.
In a battle with corsairs
There me earring was lost.

Their scimitars flashing
In the bright noonday sun
They attacked me with twelve men,
And where I… was but one.

Of course, I saw victory.
Why, that needn't be said,
But me earring, in battle,
It was freed from me head.

Aye, it's just a gold earring
But I do hold it dear,
You'll probably find it
Still attached to me ear.

Aye, and should it be found
There's just one thing I fear…
Will it look quite as manly
On me opposite ear?

෴

1.29 Softball Game Tonight

by David Alan Hoag - September 27, 2007

A scheduled game at ten-till-nine
I find a late-night starting time.

I end up working late… alone
It much too far for driving home.

The other team might find it nifty,
This later start at twenty-fifty.

Their hopeful thought: to find us stinking
From oft protracted warm-up drinking.

Last week's game gave hope anew
Of winning games for fans to view.

Though I don't know how well we'll fare,
You can count me in… I'll be there!

❧

[Some of the guys I worked with joined a recreational softball league. The name of the company was Triconex, and we made safety systems for manufacturing, fire and gas facilities, and the nuclear power industry. After several acquisitions by large holding companies, we still called ourselves Triconex, even though we were really only a small product line of a larger corporation.

Their team name, proudly emblazoned on their jerseys, was Triconex. Though the jerseys looked sharp, the team itself was anything but. Actually, most of the team felt that protracted alcohol consumption, both before and after the game, seemed to improve the perception of their game play.

I remained a staunch supporter; one of only a few.

1.30 Forgiving Heart

by David Alan Hoag – March 08, 2009

Each lash upon your bleeding back,
Was a lash you bore for me.
Each thorn, each nail, each drop of blood,
My sins… on Calvary.

You suffered there, upon that cross,
And you died that I might live.
You rose, and want a walk with me;
Jesus… teach me… to forgive.

∾

[Sometime the person that needs the most encouragement is… me. I wrote
this during a time when I was struggling with finding it hard to forgive
a rather egregious wrong. I still wander back to this poem when I need
encouragement to forgive; to be reminded that, on your own, it's difficult.]

2 Epic Poems

According to Webster's New World Dictionary, "epic is a long narrative poem in a dignified style about the deeds of a traditional or historical hero or heroes; typically, a poem like the Iliad or the Odyssey with certain formal characteristics." ... An epic is a long narrative in verse, while a ballad is a short story in verse.

The casual reader will instantly note that none of my epics come even marginally close to most traditional epic poetry. The poetic license I earned during my college days way back in 1971 grants me immunity from having to adhere to accepted norms and tropes. Essentially, any of my poems of 10 or more stanzas, or any that stretch on for 2 or more pages are likely to be deemed "epic", at least by my standards.

2.1 Gorm Grymme

Poetic Translation:
From the Ancient Fremennik by David Alan Hoag (Cigam Mai) - August 18, 2010
With Thanks to Theador Fontane

King Gorm rules o'er the Fremennik land,
For thirty years, with might,
He rules with purpose, and steady hand,
But with age, his hair's gone white,
White now's become the bushy brow,
Whose scowl makes wild-men tame,
Grim: the only visage he'll allow,
Gorm Grymme, therefore, his name.

And the Fremennik all see at the summer's feast,
Beside Gorm, a vision of life,
He is the West, and she is his East,
Thyra Danabode, his wife;
Each silently takes the other's hand
And they know without having to speak,
That their union is more than uniting the land,
Gorm Grymme, what makes you so weak?

At the end of the court at the end of the hall,
Is excitement; unfettered and wild
Young Darvald plays with the feathered ball,
Young Darvald, their only child,
His build is slim; though strong and lean,
Regal clothes of blue and white,
Young Darvald today is just fifteen,
He is the King's delight.

They love him both; but a notion of fear
Comes over the queen that day,
Gorm Grymme, motions for all to hear,
And points at young Darvald to say,
And he stands to speak, - in his mantle of red,
The symbol of all his power:
"Whoever tells me 'my son is dead',
Will die... within the hour!"

And seasons change. Summer's plain to see,
For springtime now has past,
Three hundred ships sail out to sea,
Young Darvald is at the mast,
He sails with the fleet, he sings a song,
A sword held fast in his fist,
Gorm Grymme watches the whole day long,
As sails dwindle into the mist.

And seasons change. Grey autumn's day,
As leaves fall from the tree,
Just three ships, slowly making their way,
Row homeward o'er the sea;
Veiled in black; at the end of the pier,
Young Darvald draws no breath,
Who will take the news to the King's ear?
No one would seal his death.

Thyra Danabode runs to the pier,
She had seen the sails that day;
She speaks: "You needn't fear
I will tell him in my own way."
Clouded in tears, and gasping for breath,
She takes off her royal ring,
Sadly donning a black dress of death,
And enters the Hall of the King.

Hung in the Hall, by the King's command,
Tapestries of gold and red,
Black draperies, now, by her own hand,
The Queen hangs in their stead,
Twelve candles are lit; they give scant light,
Rubs ash in her golden hair,
She lays a shroud, the color of night,
Over young Darvald's chair.

In walks Gorm Grymme. Soft his steps fall,
He walks as in a dream,
He stares the length of the mighty Hall,
The lights cast a ghostly sheen.
Gorm Grymme speaks: "The air here feels dead,
Let us go to sea and strand,
Fetch me my cloak of gold and of red
And let me have your hand."

She gave him a cloak, dark and gray,
It was not golden, not red,
Gorm Grymme sobs: "What none will say,
I speak it: 'He is dead.'"
He sinks to the floor, too weak to stand,
A chill wind blows about,
The king and the queen clutch each other's hand,
The candles flicker out.

᷍

[Cigam Mai was the name of the avatar (character) I played in RuneScape (an online game). I actually created a poetic translation of Theador Fontane's poem by the same name that was originally written in German way back in 1864. I translated it, brought it back into a poetic form, and modified it only slightly to fit the Fremennik history of the RuneScape universe where I first published it on clan pages in 2010.]

2.2 Accidental Causes

By David Alan Hoag - June 6, 2017

There's a busy intersection
In Dublin, by the bay.
That is a source of bad luck, and
Vehicular dismay.

Last year, when we left Denica's
With Jeff and Bob in tow,
They said: "Can we go to a park?"
Then Grammie said: "Let's go."

As we hit the intersection
Of Dougherty and Dublin
The light was red, and so I stopped…
Then started up again.

Turning right on red is legal,
We do it every day,
But here, where these streets intersect
They'll fine you; make you pay.

"But Officer, we saw no sign."
My plea fell on deaf ears.
"It's across six lanes of traffic;
The sign's been there for years."

Well, that was fun. Three hundred bucks
Spent better on the boys,
Instead, a secret Dublin tax
Decreased our Sunday joys.

This year… we were in a park, in
The hills of San Ramon
Acres of fun, a zip-line, too,
And awesome kid-a-phone.

Great fun was had with hide-and-seek,
As Mom joined in their game
The boys wished Pop-Pop would join in,
But sadly, he was lame.

The splashing water feature died
The day was in retreat.
And we'd all worked up a hunger
"So… come on, let's go eat."

When we left for Rigatoni's
With Jeff and Bob in tow,
Their Mom said: "There's a faster way"
To get there that I know."

Dublin and Dougherty, once again;
The intersection loomed.
We felt a chill, and tried to laugh;
Our fate already doomed.

We're now aware: DON'T TURN ON RED!
So patiently we wait.
Someone steps into the crosswalk
With slow and lumb'ring gait.

Though now it's green, we may not turn
My daughter does remind.
And as the walker saunters by
We're rammed from the behind!

A newly minted driving teen
Whose foot slipped off the brake,
Or something else, who quite can tell?
At best, a sad mistake.

This spot seems cursed; a bad-luck cloud
Would make our lives undone.
Yet, as we inspect the damage
It's minimal, or none.

Examining this wretched luck
It really gives me pause.
When I look at all the reasons
My grandsons… seem the cause.

[We love breakfast at Denica's Real Food Kitchen, just north of the fateful intersection. Rancho Park is in hills of San Ramon, north of Denica's, and a bit to the west, Rigatoni's serves delightful Italian food. You've been warned, so BEWARE the fateful intersection!]

2.3 The Art of a Muse

By David Alan Hoag - January 12, 2017

Great art, like our Yana
With each shade of light
Mercurial talent,
Seductive and bright.

I see in *From the Lake*
O'Keeffe's wondrous range
The light on the ripples
A summer of change.

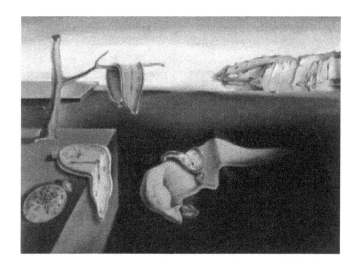

Dali taught me that time
In life, or in dreams
Is a quite surreal thing
And not what it seems.

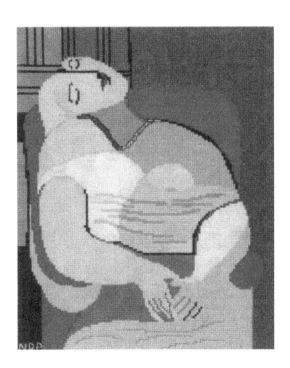

Oh, and speaking of dreams
Pablo caught her face
In a faraway thought
In some cubic space.

Monet's inspiration?
A calm garden sight
Creates an impression
Of color and light.

And Vincent, dear Vincent
Bathed in terrace light
Has drawn in our eye with
A bright starry night.

And Vermeer, the master
With turn of the head,
Caught uncertain future
In one to be wed.

Renoir paints a luncheon
Beside the Seine stream;
One girl lost in distance.
Of what does she dream?

In the gold of a dream
And time out of place
Klimt wraps up his lovers
In passion's embrace

Gazing out like Yana's
Enigmatic smile
Makes me think Da Vinci
Knew her for a while.

[Yana Reznik, a recognized muse, published a picture of herself, something she does frequently. But this time it was adjacent to a Facebook post about some of the greatest paintings in the world. The 2 things planted a seed, and I started this work in February of 2014, picked it up from time to time, and finally completed it in January of 2017. The poem may not qualify in length as an epic poem, but it sure does qualify as an epic amount of time to finally bring it together.

In no way can black and white representations of these pieces of great art do them justice. I suggest seeing them in person for best effect. If travelling to museums around the world is not in your current budget, you should at least look them up online.]

3 IAMBIC PENTAMETER

Iambic pentameter is a type of metric line used in traditional English poetry and verse drama. The term describes the rhythm, or meter, established by the words in that line; rhythm is measured in small groups of syllables called "feet". Each line of verse has five metrical feet, each consisting of one short (or unstressed) syllable followed by one long (or stressed) syllable, for example: "Two households, both alike in dignity."

3.1 Glimmering Hope

by David Alan Hoag - June 7, 2011

'Twas but a season that we strived anon
And labored to increase but three percent,
While reaching for the prize, we hastened on
And by "a prize" we wondered what was meant.

We wondered: "Was the promise just a ruse?"
Our hair… now white, our beards also gone gray;
Yet, holding onto hope is what we choose.
Lo, still… there is no prize for us this day!

[I created this short poem to prod my friend, Brad Seeley, to provide the prizes he had promised for a company promotion. All entries that suggested something that could outline an idea that might result in a 3% (or more) cost savings for the company would win a prize. My team was notified that our idea was selected as one of the winners, but many weeks had passed with no prizes being awarded. Thus, this poem was written to commemorate yet another week passing... with still no promised prize. I wrote it in iambic pentameter just for fun.]

3.2 Fourth of July

By David Alan Hoag - July 2, 2012

Red-white-and-blue banners lining the streets,
Picnics that offer such wonderful treats,
Brilliant bombardments that fill the night sky;
These are the things that say: Fourth of July.

Fireworks framing Miss Liberty's flame;
Just for the promise, in masses they came.
The tired and poor heard Liberty's call,
Not freedom for some, but freedom for all.

Cherish your freedoms, you are without doubt
Free to move freely, and free to speak out,
Freedom to try; even sometimes to lose.
Freedom to worship; however you choose.

Though we disagree, and sometimes there's strife,
We stand together to live a free life.
So raise up the flag, and strike up the band
Celebrate freedom across this great land!

3.3 For Glory

by David Alan Hoag - September 21, 2013

When I am set upon by the fair Muse,
Then greedily I clutch her to my breast;
Her presence is a gift I can't refuse.
When she is near, there is no time for rest.

I'm human, but the Muse's call I hear
And human, recognition's what I crave.
But History's drumbeat stokes my greatest fear:
Fame often finds most poets… in the grave.

I must embrace a truth, both cold and stark,
That though illumination is my goal
The vast bulk of my work falls in the dark
It's joy… if I can light up just one soul.

And while the road I travel's not oft trod
It draws me to a life I can't resist.
Though rarely does my verse receive a nod
It seems, I must for Glory, still persist.

❧

[I wrote this in iambic pentameter to thank Ylorg, a RuneScape player, for the thoughtfulness of a kind review. This was also a play on words; read "Ylorg" backwards.]

4 LIMERICKS

Limericks are one of my favorite forms of verse, and have been around since the early years of the 18th century. They seem to come naturally to me, and I am moved to create them for all manner of occasions. Quite often, my limericks honor people and everyday situations (though some might say that there's a fine line between mocking and honoring). My limericks are usually humorous and sometimes ribald. The technical definition of a limerick is a verse written in five-line, predominantly anapestic meter with a strict rhyme scheme of AABBA, in which the first, second, and fifth line rhyme, while the third and fourth lines are shorter and share a different rhyme. The following example is a limerick of unknown origin:

> The limerick packs laughs anatomical
> Into space that is quite economical.
>> But the good ones I've seen
>> So seldom are clean
> And the clean ones so seldom are comical.

Note that limericks have a strict meter. Lines 1, 2, and 5 have seven to ten syllables (three metrical feet) and rhyme with one another. Lines 3 and 4 have five to seven syllables (two metrical feet) and also rhyme with each other. The rhyme scheme is usually "A-A-B-B-A".

Limericks also have a distinct rhythm. The rhythm is as follows:

da **DUM** da da **DUM** da da **DUM**	7-10 syllables A
da **DUM** da da **DUM** da da **DUM**	7-10 syllables A
da **DUM** da da **DUM**	5-7 syllables B
da **DUM** da da **DUM**	5-7 syllables B
da **DUM** da da **DUM** da da **DUM**	7-10 syllables A

What follows are a few of the many limericks I've written over the years.

4.1 On Vacation

David Alan Hoag - December 16, 2011

Dave Hoag, as you see, is not here.
If you need him, you might shed a tear.
> For he's gone far away,
> With his grandsons to play,
And he shan't be returning this year!

4.2 Diversity

David Alan Hoag - September 14, 2011

Though limericks might cause you to curse
There is meter and rhyme to my verse.
        Although born "black and white"
        In full color I might
Show characters much more diverse!

4.3 Adam's Birthday

David Alan Hoag - January 24, 2012

Your birthday; don't mope and don't whine.
Just look how your life is so fine!
      An artistic wizard,
      Now working for Blizzard,
And soon, they will let your art shine!

[Written for Adam Portillo, artist extraordinaire, on his birthday.]

4.4 Shower Challenge

David Alan Hoag - June 23, 2007

Well, Jenny's not one to be coy
While she carries her new baby boy
      She loves Oscar a bunch
      But I have a good hunch
That Jeffrey's her new pride and joy.

∾

[Written after my wife, Patti, and my youngest daughter, Wendy, challenged me to produce a limerick (a game they had played at a shower they threw for my pregnant oldest daughter, Jennifer).]

4.5 Treasure

David Alan Hoag - February 2, 2012

I'm never depressed or forlorn.
For power and wealth I don't mourn.
  I got all life's pleasure,
  And wealth beyond measure,
The day my sweet daughters were born!

[Written for my daughter, Jennifer Jerkins, on her birthday. Included, of course, was my other daughter, Wendy Portillo.]

4.6 Nick's Birthday

David Alan Hoag - March 15, 2012

A slippage of schedule's not new;
We know you've delivered late, too.
  But we got you a card,
  And we hired a bard
To wish Happy Birthday to you!

❧

[A Birthday limerick for Nick Houlbrook… a day after his actual Birthday.]

4.7 Limerick for David Lappa

David Alan Hoag - July 3, 2012

Though his poem is a bit of a crime,
We still give him a pass all the time.
    For he covers you see
    All that tough V&V
It's a shock! Who knew Lappa could rhyme?

❧

[In response to my 4th of July poem, David Lappa, a most amazing V&V guru, inked the following:

Roses are red.
Violets are blue.
I hope you had a good
Fourth of July, too.

My limerick above is a response to David Lappa's doggerel.]

4.8 Read and Sign

Read and Sign

By David Alan Hoag - October 30, 2015

The GNP reading's my ruin;
Been on my back burner since June.
      Gary Hufton would state,
      When oft pressed for a date:
"As always, it's scheduled for SOON"!

∾

[An email had commanded me to complete some low priority reading of our Global Nuclear Procedures (GNP). For me, at least as specified by my boss, this was a very low priority task, so it elicited the above poetic response.

The "low priority" ensures that the GNP read and sign task only moves forward in fits and starts.

Besides my boss, I also sent it to Gary Hufton, the former head of R&D at Triconex, who made famous the "soon" expression. I thought he might like to see himself immortalized in verse. His response: "Thanks, I am honored."]

4.9 Scouting the Territory

By David Alan Hoag - February 16, 2016

The queen of the King Cakes, one day
Came home, and was angered to say:
      "There's a little Girl Scout
      Who just waits till I'm out;
Sells my husband her quota each day!"

❦

[My good friend, Barbara Scalia, sent our office a couple of King Cakes from Haydel's Bakery in New Orleans every year just before Fat Tuesday. This limerick was inspired by a Facebook picture and post by Barb about how her husband Joe bought 10 boxes of Girl Scout cookies while she was out.

4.10 A Limerick for Gary Wilkinson

By David Alan Hoag - February 4, 2016

It seems, almost everyone knows
The meter that from my pen flows
  To the world it is worse
  That I publish in verse
So, I leave to you… all of the prose.

❧

[My friend, Gary Wilkinson, is a teacher, writer, author, comedian, and all around great guy. Gary's prose spans non-fiction to murder mysteries, and you can find his published works on Amazon. He sent me the following email, which made me laugh and immediately sparked the bit of poetic creativity, above. Gary's humorous message:

From: Gary Wilkinson
To: Hoag, David
Subject: Your New Novel

David,

You must keep writing! May I humbly suggest an idea for your new novel?

- Plot:
    - o   A team of engineers build a machine that can either save or destroy the world. The leaders of the team disagree on what to do with the machine.
- Conflict:
    - o   The two leaders are in love with the same woman!
- Theme:
    - o   A man struggles to overcome his fate, but cannot overcome love.

One of the unknown pleasures of writing fiction is that it also serves as a great way to settle old scores from high school. :)
I will expect a rough draft by June to review... you are the artist!

Your Friend

Gary]

4.11 SNAFU

By David Alan Hoag – April 7, 2014

There once was a Dilbert cartoon,
Depicting a management goon,
      Who had been such a jerk
      When he caused a STOP WORK
His team kicked him clear to the moon!

4.12 A Limerick for Mark Lehman

By David Alan Hoag - September 25, 2016

Mark Lehman, not over the hill
His tee shots are always a thrill
     Hear his golf course reply
     With "Here's mud in your eye!"
He's golfing and cycling still.

⇛

[Mark Lehman and I have been good friends for a very long time. Mark was one of the first to purchase my book, *Sharing Christmas*, and when he finally got around to bringing the book by, I signed it with the above limerick.

While working together at Hughes Aircraft in Fullerton, California, we would spend our lunch hours playing a quick round of disc golf at a nearby course. A beautiful disc golf course threads its way through La Mirada Regional Park, with concrete tee pads and professional disc golf baskets. A leaking sprinkler pipe had caused a large, muddy area to form right in front of the tee pad for the 8th hole. As Mark's follow-through usually carried him off the end of the tee pad, I suggested that he try a more toned-down launch off the tee. Mark indicated that I should mind my own business, did his usual run-up, and promptly slipped off the end of the pad… right into the mud. I was laughing so hard (Mark later described it as a cackle) that I was doubled over and in tears. Covered in mud, Mark was not appreciating the humor of the situation as much as I was, so he scooped up a handful of mud while I was doubled over with laughter, walked up to me, and smacked the mud into me as if he was giving me a pie in the face! That stopped my laughter!!! Sputtering and wiping the mud away, I was more surprised than angry. OK, I was a little angry, but that soon gave way to both of us laughing at how ridiculous the situation had become. It's one of those memories that will remain crystal clear… and precious to us… forever.]

4.13 A Limerick for Omed Muzaffrey

By David Alan Hoag - September 20, 2012

A handsome young man named Omed,
Took many young ladies to bed.
...They'd line up for a mile,
...And leave with a smile,
In whispers, all sighing: OH...med!

[An actual ribald limerick. No real evidence to back up the claim, but
Omed never denied it.]

4.14 Omed Moved

By David Alan Hoag - November 16, 2012

Omed's tenure here has now ceased;
Not laid-off, nor is he deceased.
> You won't have to look far,
> His coordinates are…
A cubical to the southeast.

[Omed's cubical used to be located next to mine, but he had been moved a few cubicles, but still in our area. I posted this limerick on his old cubical to alert people. I fear for humanity, as, as most of the people still asked about Omed, thinking either that he had died, or had quit. Since people couldn't find him, he discovered that, for a while at least, he could classify himself as R.I.P. (Really Increased Productivity).]

4.15 For Allen Barker

By David Alan Hoag - August 18, 2011

Allen came here decades ago
And there's one thing people here know
     Through the sunshine and rain
     And the pain… of a train…
The inmate is running the show.

ॐ

[A limerick for Allen Barker's 25th Anniversary at Triconex.]

4.16 Currency of the Dead

By David Alan Hoag - August 26, 2013

I currently work like a slave,
A struggling project to save.
      While they pay overtime,
      I don't see the sunshine.
Can I spend the OT from the grave?

[The eternal question: Is overtime worth it?]

4.17 FBC Pickers

By David Alan Hoag – August 12, 2011

These folks sure do teach a fine lesson:
With music, their faith they're confessin'.
     See… there's no need to shout,
     Or thump Bibles about;
These Pickers are really a blessin'!

₨

[My Friend, Monica Martin, is bass player in a musical group called The FBC Pickers. They were about to play a new gig, and I was moved to write a promotional limerick for the event. I'd be surprised if the limerick was seen by more than a handful of people on Facebook. The Pickers, however, can be seen live around the Guntersville, AL area. You can also see them perform on YouTube.]

4.18 What Prize?

By David Alan Hoag – June 14, 2012

As the hope slowly fades from my eyes
And my faith in humanity dies;
      Back in April, for fun
      A submission I won.
Now it's June, and I still have no prize.

[My Earth day submission supposedly won a prize. I really didn't care about the prize. I just loved poking the bear.]

4.19 Muscovy Duck

By David Alan Hoag – April 15, 2013

"It's a turkey," said Jan, quite awestruck.
But in truth, it's a Muscovy duck.
      Twice as big as an owl,
      This red-faced water fowl.
The turkey… is HOLDING the duck!

[Janice Palmer sent me the following picture of Dave Waterman, and challenged me to write a poem. This limerick is the result.]

4.20 Twister

By David Alan Hoag - May 20, 2013

I hear the Midwest oft transforms
When weather its tantrums performs.
      Oklahoma, I hear,
      Has tornados to fear;
I pray you're all safe from the storms!

[I had no relatives in the Midwest; my prayers were for all my friends who were concerned for the safety of their families.]

4.21 Time Off

By David Alan Hoag - August 8, 2012

Your eyes will be tired and blurry.
Remember when driving, don't hurry.
  Take your daughters and son
  And make memories of fun;
Relax, decompress, and don't worry!

൙

[My friend and co-worker, Steve Harris, was leaving for a short vacation. As usual, work had piled up at the last moment, so I sent him this limerick, along with the following:

Steve,
Have a great time on vacation. Don't worry about anything… it'll ALL be here when you return! I promise not to accomplish anything while you are gone.]

4.22 Beans? Again?

By David Alan Hoag - March 20, 2013

A cow... Jack was told he must sell.
He got beans. Said his mom: "What the hell?!?
      OPC, you pea-brain?
      Are you crazy-insane?
Bechtel... Software for free, I foretell.

❧

[We had a customer demand that we set up and install a complicated software package they had us buy for them, but they declined to pay for any software support. They wanted us to prove the software package to be working during final testing, without paying us to set up their architecture. Unbelievably, this was happening again.

What is OPC?
OPC is the interoperability standard for the secure and reliable exchange of data in the industrial automation space and in other industries. It is platform independent and ensures the seamless flow of information among devices from multiple vendors.

Initially, the OPC standard was restricted to the Windows operating system. As such, the acronym OPC was born from OLE (object linking and embedding) for Process Control. These specifications, which are now known as OPC Classic, have enjoyed widespread adoption across multiple industries, including manufacturing, building automation, oil and gas, renewable energy and utilities, among others.

With the introduction of service-oriented architectures in manufacturing systems came new challenges in security and data modeling. The OPC Foundation developed the OPC UA specifications to address these needs and at the same time provided a feature-rich technology open-platform architecture that was future-proof, scalable and extensible.
Today the acronym OPC stands for Open Platform Communications.]

4.23 Failure Modes and Effects Analysis

By David Alan Hoag - March 15, 2013

The F-M-E-A was some fun,
And though I am technically done,
    With the time that I've spent
    Feeling broken and bent,
I really don't feel like I've won!

∽

[As you might expect, Failure Modes and Effects Analysis for nuclear safety systems are challenging and time consuming.]

4.24 Limerick Power

By David Alan Hoag - November 25, 2011

From the air, Limerick's towers are keen
And its nuclear power is green.
     For hour after hour
     It's the safest of power;
Pennsylvania is where they are seen.

[We didn't get the Limerick contract, but I did get inspired to write a poem about the Limerick Generating Station in Pennsylvania. The facility has two General Electric boiling water reactor (BWR) units, cooled by natural draft cooling towers. The two units are capable of producing over 1,200 megawatts of power, which combined can provide electricity to over 2 million households.]

4.25 Stuntman

By David Alan Hoag - June 9, 2011

Some might think it a little bit crass
That you fight with a tot you out-mass
      Yet his fearless attack
      Brings a whole lot of smack;
I've got film of him kicking your ass!

∾

[This limerick commemorates a whole lot in five short lines.

We have a weekly tradition of eating at a favorite Mexican Restaurant in Yorba Linda, California called Joaquin's. It's located in a strip mall, right next to a small plaza, ringed with benches, with four good-sized patches of lush grass in the center. Since Joaquin's is very popular, we usually had to wait a few minutes for a table. Often, we waited outside the restaurant, on the plaza.

Our tradition started with two families, and over the decades, the number of people at dinner waxed and waned. Children grew up, moved out, came back to visit, brought friends, and… eventually… brought grandchildren. This limerick commemorates a period of time when both our families had a grandson in tow each week. Michael Krausman was the teenage grandson of our friends, and the other was our 3-year old grandson, Jeffrey. Jeffrey loved chasing Michael around on the grass while we waited. If Jeffrey caught up with him, Michael would allow himself to be tackled, making Jeffrey believe he could actually take down a towering teenager. Michael had a whole bag of tricks that would put many a stuntman to shame. He made it look like Jeffrey could grab his arm and throw him through the air. If Jeffrey pushed him, Michael would fling himself backward and into the air, landing flat on his back. The plaza was filled with laughter and giggles, and it was pretty infectious for anyone passing by. Through his tumbling, flipping, and falling, Michael gave Jeffrey a great gift of confidence, courage, and persistence.]

5 COMMEMORATIVE POEMS

A commemorative poem is a way for me to take a snapshot of a moment in time, an emotion, a special place, or a unique event, and enshrine it in my poetic universe. Typically, poems in this section commemorate something memorable or wonderful.

I have written many poems commemorating death and the passing of friends and loved ones, but they have been grouped in the next section, called "In Memoriam".

5.1 Lunar Dreams

By David Alan Hoag - July 21, 2009

"You won't reach the moon!" the critics would say.
It seems, where angels fear, you'll oft find fools.
Fools with poor computers to chart their way
The tools back then: engineering slide rules.

The Russians claimed a scientific win,
But a grander goal, Kennedy would tout:
"Easy to orbit some sputnik-type tin,
But we'll walk on the moon, by ten years out!"

Amazingly, we've proven that we can
Pursue, and yes, catch the dreams of our mind
By our self, it's: "One small step for a man,"
Together: "One giant leap for mankind!"

Here's to the millions of people who shared
As they listened at home or in their cars
Though humans may be by gravity snared,
We look up and dream of flights to the stars.

Forty years later, where did it go wrong?
Space-junk... high over clouds of white cotton;
Footprints left by Commander Neil Armstrong;
The Moon's great promise... all but forgotten.

There's no indication or any sign
That men will walk in the lunar dust soon,
But, the summer of nineteen-sixty-nine
We saw men walk on the face of the moon.

Our fate is not to be safe; it would seem.
Our destiny is really so much more.
We take that small step, deciding to dream;
We make that giant leap… when we explore!

[Written to commemorate the 40th anniversary of man's first steps on the Moon.]

5.2 In the Hurricane's Wake

by David Alan Hoag - January 5, 2014

I wake now to a house that's calm;
No body-slamming boys
To budge this world-dead sleeping log
With: "Pop-pop, fix our toys!"

I shuffle through the living room.
Why aren't I filled with joy?
For now my toes no longer ache
Stubbed; bleeding by some toy.

The kitchen floor is clear again;
No wooden blocks to kick.
But more amazing, I suppose…
My bare feet now don't stick!

No doors are slammed, no balls are thrown,
No shades knocked off their lamps.
No shouting, screaming, screeching play,
No sticky-fingered scamps.

Now, once again, I sit and read
Without a lap that's sore
From reading to a little boy
Demanding: "Just one more?!?"

Their visit's done, and all's now back
To where it needs to go.
Chaos is gone, order restored,
And yet… I miss them so!

❧

5.3 A Father's Questions

by David Alan Hoag - February 2, 2014

How is it that you've filled our house
Yet again with blocks and toys,
And chaos... and the shrieks of joy
From your precious little boys?

How is it that I walked the aisle
And then let him take your hand,
To pledge his love... and yours to him...
With a golden wedding band?

How is it I survived the nights
Where behind the door I'd wait,
In fevered, wild imaginings...
Were you just one minute late?

How is it that the local schools
Were the options you'd refuse,
The distance, parties, or the slugs...
Why pick Santa Cruz?

How is it that you learned to run;
That YOU... diving in the pool?
From Kindergarten to Twelfth Grade,
Are you suddenly through school?

How is it that the tiny child
Newborn, and sent from heaven,
And always still my little girl...
This day turns thirty-seven?

൭

[Inspired by, and written for my oldest daughter, Jennifer Jerkins, on her birthday. With love, Pop.]

5.4 The Real Diehl

by David Alan Hoag - March 9, 2014

Rare indeed, a love so deep;
Not commitment, chore, or duty.
Instead, a focus most can't see,
He saw your inner beauty.

Far beyond your shaping world
He could see a future glowing
He loved the you… that you would be;
A rare, discerning, knowing.

"Encouraging is easy,"
He'd chuckle with a grin,
"And more so when your heart will see
Their gifts, locked deep within."

The secret that will unlock
The gifts God gave to you and me?
Just emulate what Diehl had done:
Encouragement's the key.

♫

[Monica was Diehl Martin's beautiful and talented lady, special in his eyes. The more I knew Diehl, the more I came to understand that he saw EVERYONE with that same special discernment.]

5.5 Send-off

by David Alan Hoag - April 20, 2014

You all have gone, well more or less,
Though... always growing is the mess,
And for what's left behind, I'd guess,
We'll ship it up... by UPS.

I hate it when we have to part,
So, ere you get too big a start...
Like thieves, you've practiced well your art...
And once again, you've stole... my heart!

✒

[Written just as my eldest daughter and her family (Jennifer and Henry Jerkins, along with Jeffrey Delgado and Bob Jerkins) left after their Easter visit. When the grandsons come for a visit, our neat and ordered life dissolves into constant uproar and chaos; I love it!]

5.6 Citizen Soldier

By David Alan Hoag - October 10, 2001

Citizen Soldier, Citizen Brother
Your family…
And fellow citizens…
Salute you, thank you, and pray for you.

We salute you…
Salute you for being one of the best…
Salute you for submitting to training few can endure…
Salute you for standing tall and proud…
Salute you for choosing to defend the security and the freedoms of our country.

We thank you…
Thank you for serving your unit…
Thank you for serving the military…
Thank you for serving a grateful nation…
Thank you for serving a world, which oftentimes seems ungrateful.

For you, we pray…
Pray that God's hand be upon you…
Pray that God's protection surround you…
Pray that God grant you courage, strength, and resolve…
Pray that God tempers you with wisdom, mercy, and kindness.

Never forget…
Never forget who you are…
Never forget who, and what, you represent…
Never forget the words of Abraham Lincoln, who said:
"With malice toward none…
With charity for all…
With firmness in the right as God gives us to see the right…
Let us strive on to finish the work we are in…
To bind up the nation's wounds…
To care for him who shall have borne the battle
And for his widow and his orphan…
To do all which may achieve and cherish a just and lasting peace…
Among ourselves…
And with all nations."

෴

[Written to celebrate Ian Hoag's graduation from Navy Seal training on October 10th, 2001. And yes, I'm very proud to have a Navy Seal in the family! Ian is my Dad's Uncle's boy. I think that makes him a cousin of some kind. Whatever you call it, I call it AWESOME!!!]

5.7 The Clueless Father of Daughters

by David Alan Hoag - June 18, 2012

Of all the difficult things in your life,
Of the many trials that you've had,
I'm sure that the toughest to overcome
Was to suffer... with me as your dad.

Too loud and too brash, too often uncool;
Always demanding perfection.
Reminding you how to do it "just so"
When you didn't want ANY direction.

How could a person just not understand?
Claim only logical dealings?
You wondered: "Could he be really that dense?"
"Can he NOT see the pain of my feelings?!?"

I know that I pondered riddles too much,
And it drove you quite crazy, when...
I'd get my props, and you'd cry to your Mom:
"He's about to do magic, again!"

Perhaps I could have answered everything
Instead of just making life hell:
"Why are you asking me to help you out?
There's a Dictionary... to help you spell."

I was the crazy, competitive dad
That read all the rules, all the time.
Checking the rules, they would protest and moan
You'd think I'd committed some heinous crime.

I know some things anger you to this day,
Though still I proclaim far and wide
The passing of time can't dull or contain
That I'm still "busting my buttons" with pride!

It's lucky for you; I did one thing right,
One thing over every other:
I may not have gotten everything right,
But I married your wonderful mother!

5.8 Thanksgiving Reflections

By David Alan Hoag - November 16.2007

In ages past, Thanksgiving Day
Brought thanks from employees
Whose bosses gave them Turkey Cards;
"A Bird"... that's sure to please!

As time went by, the coupon changed.
Not good for just a bird,
But also could be used to buy
Most vittles for your herd.

So now... we have a plastic card,
With no restrictive clause.
It's good at stores... for anything,
Which really gives me pause

With choices all throughout the stores
How will I ever choose?
Perhaps I'll celebrate in style
And spend it all on booze!

[Written in appreciation of our Thanksgiving gift card]

5.9 Magic

By David Alan Hoag - July 24, 2012

I'm a magician.
    I know truths few others are even dimly aware of.

People don't want the truth.
The truth is usually boring,
And mostly made up of long hours and hard work.

People want the illusion...
        Something from nothing...
        Make the unpleasantness disappear...
        Make the impossible seem,
            Not just probable,
                But within easy grasp.

People love to be astounded!

෴

5.10 Knocking

by David Alan Hoag - January 29, 2014

God steers me to his purpose
With words I need to hear;
Often, when I hear God's Word,
It comes from Paul Lanier.

You don't need to know the name
Of every tiny sprout,
Nor the number of the stalks,
Or heads they each bring out.

No need to count the kernels;
There's only one real need:
Heed and speak the Word of God...
And keep on planting seed.

❧

[Paul Francis Lanier, a spiritual mentor and friend, posted the following on Facebook, which inspired the above poem.

"Went through my computer last night and deleted hundreds of email addresses. Some from names I don't even recognize. Others from folk I haven't spoken to in years. No doubt some had abandoned their old tired address years ago, but not me. I should have removed them long, long ago. A thousand reasons why I'd kept them . . . but none of them were good enough anymore. You see, I don't let go easily, it's just who I am. **But there comes a time when you must stop looking down the road and start listening to the door at those who've been knocking for too long, waiting for a home in your heart."**

Paul touches many people with God's Word; people who don't rub elbows with him on a regular basis, but have received a word, a blessing, or an invitation. Many might have only heard Paul's voice on an audio recording, read his writing, or seen a re-posted quote. Paul lives out and shares the love of Christ in a very real and honest way that draws people to him.

And though he might collect a great many email addresses, it would be impossible to stay current and connected to all the hearts he has touched. I'm OK with Paul purging my email address. Paul must be true to his calling, and his calling is not to maintain a dusty email list. It's up to us to seek out, encourage, and support the spiritual mentors (prophets) that God brings into our lives.]

5.11 It Seemed So Easy

by David Alan Hoag - July 28, 2016

I have
Visual Acuity
Which means
They verified I see.

I've trained
And read until I'm blue
All lists
And specs, and R-A-U.

I've worked
Forty years to the day
And have
A lovely resume.

They'll want,
I have a sneaking sense,
Yet more
Objective evidence.

I can't
Supply the thing they need
Because
They're asking me to bleed.

They might
Not ever sign for me
Because
We've lost reality!

⊰

[This poem was written to commemorate the "supposedly" EASY qualification as a tester. RAU, by the way, is Read And Understand. The initial requirement, an eye exam, had soon ballooned out of control, AND out of touch with reality.]

5.12 Brush Strokes

by David Alan Hoag - March 29, 2013

The canvas of my life, while large,
Still has its constraint.
Though stretched and bound, it's oft filled with
Myriad hues of paint.

Anger often paints me red
I call down death above,
But just as fast, the red of hate
Becomes the red of love.

Sadness can color everything
In a heavy blue.
Left unchecked, it turns to black,
An even darker hue.

Fear can stipple yellow on;
Oft cowardice to feel.
But happy, sunny yellow's hue
Bring waves of joy surreal.

Envy has me splashed in green;
A color I abhor.
Envy leads to jealously,
Which paints green all the more.

White, by itself, is newness,
and purity, as well.
Depending on your background,
It's death white does foretell.

Life would stand on black and white
To claim it guides the way.
Logic deals in black and white,
Life blends them into gray.

While color often sets the tone,
Colors run and fade.
Texture's what our friends create;
And that's where beauty's made.

While color's role is vital, it's
Not such a key part.
More important, are my friends;
Their brushstrokes etch my heart.

5.13 Glitter and Glue

by David Alan Hoag - June 19, 2018

You've oft been the glue
On the page of our life
To hold things together
Through troubles and strife

And I had big dreams
To stand out from the crowd
Pouring down on our life
A glittering cloud

But glitter is blown
Sometimes shaken away
Yet what merged with the glue
Had power to stay

A pattern of us
From the glitter and glue
Has emerged through the years
Still me loving you.

✌

[On this day, June 19, 1971, Patti and I were married in a little church in Los Alamitos, CA. This poem was written to commemorate that happy occasion… 47 years later.]

5.14 To My Lover

By David Alan Hoag - March 11, 1970

Emeralds shining in the day,
Or glowing in the night,
Compare not with my lover's eyes
That sparkle, oh, so bright.

If rubies are her lips,
Then hers are rubies fine,
Those same fine lips that tell me
That forever she is mine.

But these lines are so futile
For like the flight of birds,
How can I describe such grace?
For I love her more than words.

[Written for the lovely young woman who would become my wife in June of 1971.]

5.15 Hard Rock Valentine

by David Alan Hoag – February 01, 1985

Long ago
In a sunny southern land,
A man and a woman
Shared a golden wedding band.

From the River of Life
So mysterious and deep
They shared a single cup,
Which brought on vision-sleep

In the river, on its bed
Two rocks butted, head to head.
The big one had a smallish groove
The small was shiny, round, and smooth.
Small rock rolled from side to side
While big rock took it all in stride.
It came to pass, that over time
The rocks had fit together fine
And should the current surge or run,
The two rocks acted now as one.
Yet, take the small rock, as a test,
You'll see, alone it's like the rest.
And the big rock now, without the small
Doesn't seem quite right at all.
The hole where once the small rock rolled
Is empty, desolate, and cold.
Separate, they were just alone.
Together, they had built a home.

Those lovers woke
And even now,
You can hear their laughter.
Their love is strong
And they still live
Happily ever after!

[Written to my wife for Valentine's Day.]

5.16 William and Kate

by David Alan Hoag - April 29, 2011

As pageantry and cheering swells,
The ringing of the Abbey bells
Proclaims that all the vows were said,
So William now to Kate is wed.
Hence, with the choirs, all now sing:
"God save the future Queen and King."

[I wrote this for all my British friends, as I celebrated with them, shared in their joy of the special wedding day, and offered up my humble tribute to the royal couple.]

5.17 Unseen Power

by David Alan Hoag – June 15, 1997

White clouds brush the bottom of the sky
As bright sails rush headlong over white-tipped waves.
Misty rain, dancing with a rainbow
Forms a bridge between sea and sky

Where seagulls cavort and dance on wing tips.

Unseen, the wind gives
Direction… to clouds and rain,
Power… to the sails, and
Support… to the gulls.

Thank you for bringing wind into my life!

[One of my forays into free verse.]

5.18 American Life: Power

by David Alan Hoag - March 09, 1987

There was a time, not long ago
When the railroads did not run.
When the hand of man
Across the land
Was warmed by just the sun.

Then wood we burned to heat the steam
And the land was laid to waste,
As from wood to coal
More power we stole,
While the spinning dream we chased.

The age of man had come to be
And we worshiped the machine.
We raged on steam
But then the dream
Was changed by gasoline.

Now at last the world was ours.
Great engines ruled the land.
We flew in planes,
Or rode in trains;
Whatever our demand.

We floated mighty airships
Upon an azure sky,
Then lit the night
With neon light
Our deeds to glorify.

A slow decay had come to weigh
Upon a blighted world.
Exhaust and flue
Left residue
That billowed blew and swirled.

We dance to a malevolent Jinn,
Still we refuse to see.
Change by the hour,
Look...fusion power!
Our god, Technology.

[Written to commemorate a Thomas Hart Benton work that appeared in the EE Times fine art captioning contest. Part of a larger mural, and depicted above, it is titled *Instruments of Power*.]

5.19 A Line for Dad's Seventieth

by David Alan Hoag - June 28, 1999

For your birthday, this year, many lines I have shown.
Seventy lines, mark your years as they've flown.

Each line shows a year, for right or for wrong
Some seem way to short, while some others seem long.

Some are uneven, and some a full measure
Some a disaster, but others a pleasure.

Some are just perfect, artistic and fine,
While some miss the mark, and seem hardly a line

But taken together not viewed just in part,
They uncover the pattern of love in your heart.

❧

[I had just written "Happy Birthday, Dad" on the envelope of his birthday card, and then decided to surround that with 70 lines… one for each of his 70 years. It resembled a heart, inspired this poem, and looked like this:]

5.20 Stopping by Triconex on a Rainy Evening

by David Alan Hoag - October 19, 2004
(with apologies to Robert Frost)

Who's out sourcing? I think I know.
His office is in Foxboro though;
He will not hear me as I scream
To watch our valued IP go.

The little voice inside of me
Is wondering what the plan could be.
How can we bet our future on
The country with the lowest fee?

To build it safe, we've fought that fight
We've always kept THAT end in sight.
On some impoverished, far-off shore
Where is their will to do it right?

When safety turns on lowest pay,
And making quotas rules the day,
I've miles to go to get away,
I've miles to go to get away.

[This poem is obviously a parody of Robert Frost's famous poem (Stopping by the Woods on a Snowy Evening). I wrote it to make a statement about the hidden dangers of out sourcing our critical Safety System Intellectual Property to other countries... half a world away.]

5.21 Santa Ana Winds

by David Alan Hoag - January 31, 2018

Wind driven tumbleweeds against a fence,
Spectating along the edge of the golf course.

Trees shaking off the dust and the rust,
In strenuous calisthenics to the rhythm of the wind.

Fields of wheat doing a coordinated wave
In response to the wind's cheerleading bellows.

Dusty messengers from the desert speeding toward the beaches,
Scouring the sky clean in their wake.

Whirlwinds collecting flotsam and jetsam,
To sort into neat piles of leaves, papers, and debris.

Children gleefully imagining
That the wind will pick them up and blow them away.

Truckers arrogantly believing themselves impervious,
Find their rigs toppled by the mischievous wind.

Flags, banners, and pennants all stand at attention,
Acknowledging the great rank of the passing wind.

Tall Mexican Fan Palms swaying to a wailing beat,
High-fiving each other in their exuberant dance.

A lone seagull
Flying over the river bed into the teeth of the wind,
Flapping furiously but making absolutely no headway;
Imagining it's a hummingbird, hovering in place.

5.22 Be My Valentine

by David Alan Hoag - February 14, 2018

On Valentine's Day
Sweets couldn't miss
And "Please be mine."
Often got a kiss.

Now we've got grandkids
Nothing's the same
I'm oft confused
By a brand new game.

Now I can't bring sweets,
They're now taboo.
And pretty jewels?
They just anger you.

And a card filled up
With hearts and such?
It's now a waste
'Cause it costs too much.

A pretty trinket
Just makes you mutter:
"Have you forgot?
We're ditching clutter."

So, I've got no sweets,
I've got no hearts;
Just got our life,
All the bits and parts.

Just our life filled up
With crazy stuff
I don't need more
Because love's enough.

❧

5.23 Witnessed by Clowns

by David Alan Hoag - March 15, 1990

A cannon now signals
The start of the show
A quick transformation
To what? They don't know.

And off in the shadows
The ringmaster nods
And smiles as he works with
A handful of clods.

Empowered, he sends them
All rushing about.
A brash one, a shy one,
A big brutish lout.

With white-face and grease paint
In baggy old clothes;
They sit in the church pews
The very last rows.

As the clowns are then called,
They join in the fun.
Show: Father, Son, Spirit,
Three beings in one.

They show us they've strayed down
Temptation's false road,
But God can forgive us
And lighten our load.

Then the clowns brewed a storm
To break through the malaise
With hugging and laughing
And passing the Peace.

The clowns thought they might preach
A sermon or two,
But decided instead
To show what we do.

So they brought in some wood.
Portrayed you and me;
And with hammer and nails
Hung Christ from a tree.

"He is dead," read their sign
And alone we fail,
For all of our talents
Come to no avail.

"He is risen," said one
"Here's a sign from above!"
Now there's naught you can't do
With His gracious love.

No money for offering,
The clowns at a loss
But the offering's from God
He died on a cross.

A prayer to our Father
The blessing goes on
And just like the music
The clowns; they are gone.

And the ringmaster smiled
The whole evening long
For his clowns gave a witness
Both touching and strong.

"We need more of this here,"
They said with a frown.
If you want it, my friend,
You must first be a clown!

෧

[This poem was inspired by, and recalls a church service put on entirely by the Junior High youth. A pastor from a nearby church shared his Clown Ministry with the Youth at Redeemer Lutheran Church in Placentia, California. After being transformed into clowns, the teens led the congregation through a funny, poignant, and moving church service without speaking a word.]

5.24 Finger on the Pulse

by David Alan Hoag - December 05, 2018

The place that I work
Strives to find the best groove
So each year there's a survey
On how to improve.

Each year there's a push
To get everyone's view
But the problem's the survey's
Done by just a few.

So corporate types push
But that ends up a fail
So then managers push us
With floods of email.

"Give your opinion."
"Fill the survey out… NOW!"
"We need ALL your opinions."
"Find time, please… somehow."

Well, surveys are in
But, still, management's bent.
How'd we do on responses?
Just fifty percent.

જી

[The survey was called the Pulse Survey. Most employees thought it to be a big waste of their time. Besides being required to fill out the survey, and respond to several essay questions, there were mandatory meetings to review the prior survey, meetings to hammer home the importance of completing the survey, and meetings to schedule survey follow-up meetings. Many of us really do live in a Dilbert cartoon!]

5.25 Lake Forest Apiary

By David Alan Hoag - June 15, 2017

There's a crowd outside our doorway
They'd love to get inside.
They're looking for a place to land,
A place they might reside.

They have come because it's easy
They've heard our freedom's call.
An ineffective barrier
Has proved the mythic wall

They might have come from Mexico
Up from our southern shore,
Or from Africa invading
Still killers at their core.

They sense a hive mentality
Built up within this place;
Seems drones and workers sense the buzz,
Which sets a furious pace.

They're massing now, outside our door
And people are afraid.
Authorities are understaffed
To mount a roundup raid.

But you really needn't worry.
They'll stay out forevermore;
They just don't have the clearance for
A badge to work the door.

❧

[We had a swarm of bees outside our Lake Forest offices today.]

6 IN MEMORIAM

The following poems are memorials to friends and family that are no longer a part of this world, our communities, or our lives. There is sadness among the memories, but humor, and encouragement, too, in these memorial poems.

6.1 Michael Hoag - In Memoriam

by David Alan Hoag - June 13, 2011
(In remembrance of my brother, Michael Hoag; June 1, 1952 - April 10, 2011)

How do we each recall my brother's name?
Where, indeed, did he fit into your life?
For all of us, the answer's not the same.
Do you recall his laughter, or the strife?

Some only saw the upset and the rain
With others, he would laugh the whole day long
Some only heard his music's sweet refrain
As generously he shared his gift of song.

He definitely heard a different beat.
He oft burned bright; so too, he oft burned wild.
But… the one thing he brought to all he'd meet
Was the pure… innocent… heart of a child.

He admitted his sins; laughed at them, too.
Struggled against them with all of his might.
"How can God love me? How can that be true?"
It didn't always seem so black and white.

Mike often thought that hell might be his home,
Believing all his sins to be too grave.
The pious cite his sin; ignore their own,
And tell him he was too far gone to save.

In Matthew 12, verse 31 it's said:
"All sins will be forgiven, but for one…"
"Deny the Holy Spirit, and you're dead."
Thus spoke to us God's one and only Son.

Mike may have sinned (so at least he was taught)…
Oft he would struggle, he oft lost his way;
But, denying God's Spirit… he did not!
Know without doubt, Mike walks with God today.

❧

[When my brother Michael died, my wife suggested that I write something to share at his funeral. He and I didn't always get along, and though he openly struggled with a lot of demons in his life, he had many positive qualities. He was always struggling with guilt and feelings of not being good enough.

As I used to tell Mike, don't deny the pull of God's Spirit in your life. No matter what you think you have done, or even what you may have done, God's Spirit can cleanse you, sanctify you, and make you right and acceptable to God.

That's great news! It's wonderful to be secure in the promise that the Holy Spirit will carry us… unblemished… to heaven, to walk with God for eternity. But even better news is that if we accept Christ as our Lord and Savior today, we can walk in God's Holy Spirit here on Earth; right now! That joy is… unbelievable!

I didn't always know Christ in my life, but for the last 20 years I would share the simplicity of Christ's love with Mike whenever we talked. What I shared with Michael, I freely share with all my brothers and sisters in Christ… and in Christ we are ALL brothers and sisters. I would tell him:

> "How marvelous it is to be loved beyond all measure! How wonderful it is to know who made you, to know who loves you, to know who saves you, to know who strengthens you, to know who wants an eternal relationship with you, and to know who is coming for you! You see, that's why we worship: to celebrate that knowing!!!"]

6.2 True Quality

By David Alan Hoag - September 11, 2012
(In remembrance of Jeffrey Larson; March 7, 1960 - September 9, 2012)

Jeff Larson shared our workday life
And though, not on his team
With Jeff, you always knew that you
Were held in high esteem.

"Let's fix the problem," he would say,
"And not affix the blame."
"Let's all improve, and learn, and grow,
And not just stay the same."

A humble guy, with ready smile
Who'd stop along his way
To talk with you, and share his laugh;
Jeff brightened up our day.

His energy: all positive.
He'd lift us when we'd fall.
And he'd share his joy in passing,
Encouraging us all.

A runner... healthy, trim, and fit;
Up running with the dawn.
But none shall know the time or place,
And just like that... he's gone.

This hollow void, this sudden death;
In time, the wound will mend.
But now, my heart cries out in loss,
For Jeff... who called me "friend."

ക

[Jeff was a friend and a mentor. I still miss him.]

6.3 The Reminder

by David Alan Hoag - March 7, 2013

Lost a friend, last year, last fall
And now my phone gives me a call,
Giving in its brainless way
Reminders of my friend's birthday.

I grieve the loss of my good friend;
Our hiking days long at an end,
But in my prayers, I now can see
He's hiking through eternity.

[Remembering Jeff Larson. See *True Quality*.]

6.4 Eulogy

by David Alan Hoag - February 27, 2013

Roman's now all broken hearted;
Dave's among the dear departed
Death... missing from his failure tree
A failure mode Dave couldn't see!

But, then upon entombment day
Roman smiled, and was heard to say:
"Now Dave's within his family's vault...
The schedule slip's the dead guy's fault."

[The engineering manager of a project I was working on, was really hammering us with schedule pressures. This particular schedule was extremely tight, and the running gag was that you could only get time off if there was a death in the family - and it had better be YOUR death. I was working on the FMEA Report (Failure Modes and Effects Analysis) for the project, and it was taking longer to produce than expected; all of which became the inspiration for this short work.]

6.5 With a Whimper

By David Alan Hoag - June 11, 2012

The end is near
Of life we know
When data bits
No longer flow.

We crashed it down
Around our ears;
Now the world lays
In ruin and tears.

Who could predict
This crushing fall?
'Cause EVERYONE
Hit: "Reply All"!!!

[Written to reflect on a growing number of my peers who seem ONLY able to respond to emails with the 'Reply to All' feature.]

6.6 Me Grandma

By David Alan Hoag - March 1, 1994

Me Grandma was an Irish lass
Who traveled far from home.
At sweet sixteen she sailed away
Alone and on her own.

On foreign soil she landed,
A strange, unruly place.
Although most spoke her language,
They did so without grace.

She came to know a new land,
To marry and to love,
And by example, show us
Her faith in God above.

Her smile I still remember.
Oh, she was full of pluck.
She'd say: "It's not t' worry,
'Cause we have all the luck!"

Her heart was always open,
This grandmother of mine.
Through hurt, and pain, and suff'ring
Her Irish eyes would shine.

At the loss, although I wept
The day me Grandma died,
I know her soul's in Ireland
And God is by her side.

Irish never really leave,
Though some may travel far;
For Ireland's where their heart is
And Irish who they are.

[A poetic tribute to my Irish Grandmother, Lillian Hoag]

6.7 Phoenix Rises

by David Alan Hoag - August 15, 2016

I stand at the edge of a swift-flowing river of steel
That surges and ebbs with the pulse of the day.

Something magical has risen on the river's far bank
Framed by the last embers of the flaming sun painting the Western sky.

I expect a calm to settle over the darkening desert landscape.
I expect to see Phoenix disappear into the ash of the extinguishing sunlight.

Instead,
Phoenix rises,
Aflame in flashing light and whirling color.
Phoenix rises,
Deafening in cacophonous clanking, whirring, and ringing.

Phoenix rises,
Awash with barker enticements and promises.

Phoenix rises,
In the shining eyes of children flying off into the desert sky for the first
time.

Phoenix rises,
In the rekindled hearts of couples remembering their first heated kisses.

Phoenix rises,
In the shuffling of a thousand feet raising a cloud of sawdust memories.

Phoenix rises,
As the carnival spreads its wings, and soars
Into our reborn imagination, and heart.

❧

[In February of 2016, we spent a night in Phoenix, Arizona. We were on our way back from my sister-in-law's funeral in Tucson, and were walking into a restaurant for dinner. The carnival, across a busy street, was just cranking into life, framed by a magnificent sunset. Once I took the picture, I immediately had an idea for a poem… it just took me another six months to get it written down.]

6.8 On My Mother's Passing

by David Alan Hoag - September 13, 2019
(Barbara Jean Hoag; November 28th, 1929 - September 13th, 2019)

My mother died today with no fanfare
Watched over by my sister who was there.
Though on my way, and by the shortest route
I was, as yet, still several minutes out.

While traffic slowed my progress to a crawl
The car alerted me I had a call.
My sister's sobs hit like a driving rain:
"She's gone! Released from suffering and pain."

Just moments later I was at the bed
Not breathing, pale, and silent, she was dead.
There was a solemn stillness to Mom's face
I held my sobbing sister in embrace.

My mother died today. Though it's not fine,
She made it to the age of eighty-nine
And she'd admit, with wink and a sly grin,
Longevity past any of her kin.

She always had a smile for kin or friend,
But pain quite overwhelmed her toward end.
They gave her drugs, the horrid pain to slake
Which let her sleep, though never to awake.

She was courageous, bright and friendly, too
Quite at her best when she was feeding you
When you walked through her door, she'd always think
That you must need a cookie, meal, or drink.

To one and all, a smile she would bestow
And as she passed, there's one thing that I know:
Though towards the end she wasn't self-aware,
That she was still herself, in there somewhere.

My mother died today, and though that's sad.
There are reasons that we should still be glad:
She's free from pain and medical syndrome,
And a child of God now calls heaven home.

6.9 The Crossing

by David Alan Hoag - May 19, 1987

How can we ever know
Another's sorrow,
Especially
When one so dearly loved
Is gone?

Each of us
Stands differently
At the abyss of darkness.

The absence leaves
A yawning emptiness,
A sense of loss
Which becomes an overpowering,
Lonely
Void.

Yet, their life
Had touched ours
In so many ways.

Each touch became
A memory.
Each memory,
A shining jewel
To be held and cherished,
Never to be lost.

Memories alone
Will never completely fill
The emptiness.
But they help bridge
The chasm of our grief
And allow us to continue
Our
Lives.

To once again
Touch the lives
Of those
Who love us.

[Written for a friend who was grieving over a death in their family.]

6.10 Waving Goodbye

by David Alan Hoag - March 06, 2019

Oh, the joy!
Oh, what a day!
Mooring ropes cast off
The gangplank pulled away
The huge ship now moves from the dock
At railings, streamers make a bright collage
Well-wishers wave from shore, with "Bon Voyage!"

Oh, such joy!
Now free at last!
Pulling out to sea
The mainland shrinking fast
Your passage, already paid for
Passage such as this, you could not afford
Yet paid for you, so thus, you are aboard.

So hurried
You rushed aboard
Can you still recall
That time, all but ignored?
Those left behind may mourn and grieve
Their keening sobs a fading hue and cry
You left so fast, no time to say goodbye.

Now at sea
Peaceful tempos
No pain, no more hurt
No sorrow, no more woes
Here, every joy, onboard fulfilled.
Time slows as every day there's something new
Exotic trips, and such, for you to do.

Remember
Those left behind
On that mainland shore?
Your lives in love entwined
Their passage is, as well, assured
Now together you'll sail through seas and straits
Unhurried, for eternity awaits.

6.11 Eternity

By David Alan Hoag - August 5th, 2009

Time in its infinite span
Offers us just the merest breath.
So fleetingly we live our lives
Before we taste of death.

Monuments of marbled stone
With your last remains you entrust,
But in a few short million years
Your tomb is only dust.

In the dust of creation,
Are we just some capricious clod?
We know that we don't measure up,
Yet we are sought by God.

Adam communed in Eden
With our God, long before the fall
But don't blame Eve; it's all of us…
We heed temptation's call.

Jesus, son of the Father
His life, for all of us, he gave
In overcoming sin and death
Left just an empty grave.

Instead of raising gravestones;
In the place of struggle and strife
Decide to walk a better path…
Choose Jesus, and choose life.

❧

6.12 Requiem

by David Alan Hoag - September 26, 2014

I hope you're here to share a smile
'Cause I'm not here, you know
You want to leave? Well, feel no shame
Just get right up and go.

My Savior took away the fear
Of Reaper and of Grave.
And gave me joy, and peace, and love;
To sin… no more a slave.

So… did I share my faith with you?
My happy joyous views?
Did I share Jesus Christ with you?
And tell you the Good News?

I'm hoping you might share a laugh;
An anecdote or two,
Perhaps you'll share a heartfelt tale
Of what I meant to you.

So, if you want, reach out to me
And give my soul a lift
Embrace the love that I have known,
And take my Savior's gift!

෨

[I'd like this to be read at my own funeral. Hopefully, that is still some time off in the future.]

7 Songs

Like many Baby-Boomers, I grew up surrounded by music. My dad was an engineer who built his own Hi-Fi system. Once my mom got her music center (a lovely piece of furniture, but a rather pedestrian stereo system), dad's Hi-Fi equipment (turntable, tube-driven amplifier, and massive woofer got shoved into a bedroom with me and my brother. We would often crank up the volume to the point that the mighty woofer would rattle the windows and shake the house; *The Battle Hymn of the Republic* was one of our favorites for pure seismic activity.

Between my parent's record collection, and the collections my brother and I were amassing, we had access to a very eclectic selection of audio recordings. We listened to and enjoyed all of it. We had everything from crooners to jazz. We listened to rock-and-roll, pop, musicals, comedy, gospel, classical, blues, big band, and even some opera on old 78 LPs.

The result of all these audio recordings percolating through my brain seems to be a fairly constant stream of music and lyrics flowing through my brain and filling my thoughts in just about every situation. Now, I don't have much of a facility for actually recalling lyrics correctly, so quite naturally... I make up new ones to fit the music in my head and the situation of the moment.

If pen and paper are handy, and I'm in the mood, I'll jot down the kernel of one of these songs as I'm making it up. If the snippet of song doesn't get lost, if I work on it, take the time to craft it or fit it to the melody that is

---

driving it… it might turn into a song. Usually, I use an existing melody, as I don't seem to have any talent to either play, or write music.

If YOU have the talent to perform any of my songs that might strike your fancy, feel free to make some sort of social media recording. I'd love to see what really talented people can do with my songs. I'd appreciate it if you credit me as the author of the lyrics. Don't forget to contact me to let me know what you've done. Send me a link or an attachment. My contact information is at the back of the book.

7.1 I Am So Frozen

by David Alan Hoag - January 15, 1993
(Sung to *I'm So Lonesome I Could Cry*; with apologies to Hank Williams)

Well, my Baby used up
The water that was hot.
And if you call it lukewarm,
Well, in one word I'd say: "NOT!"

The water's so frozen, Baby,
The water's so frozen, Baby,
The water's so frozen, I could cry.

Got ice cubes on my fingers.
Got ice cubes on my toes.
And a three foot icicle
Is hanging from my nose.

'Cause I am so frozen, Baby,
'Cause I am so frozen, Baby,
'Cause I am so frozen, I could cry.

So when your Baby leaves you
No HOT water at all,
Then do the only thing you can
Inside that shower stall:

You can be frozen, Baby,
You can be frozen, Baby,
You can be frozen, 'till you die!

❧

[As you might guess, this song flowed to life while I was shivering in the shower. If you can sing while channeling Elvis, so much the better.]

7.2 Both Sides Now

by David Alan Hoag - February 28, 2015
(sung to the song of the same name, with apologies to Joni Mitchell)

Lines and lines of logic flow,
And data structures in a row,
And drivers to control I/O,
I've looked at code that way.

If FALSE is zero, TRUE is one;
A misplaced OR will stop my RUN.
So many FUNCTIONS come undone,
When code gets in my way.

I've looked at code from both sides now,
And logic makes me think somehow
It's code's illusions I recall.
I really don't know code at all.

Cover each and every case,
Ensure conditions do not race,
And be elated in the chase,
I've looked at test that way.

But now the schedule drives the show,
You're told some of your tests must go
And if you care, don't let them know,
Don't give yourself away.

I've looked at test from both sides now
From full to partial, still somehow
It's test's illusions I recall
I really don't know test at all.

Tears and fears and feeling proud,
To say "Triconex" right out loud
Dreams and schemes and conference crowds,
I've looked at us that way.

But now our customers act strange,
They shake their heads, they say we've changed.
Well something's lost, but something's gained
Each acquisition day.

I've looked at us, we've changed somehow:
Siebe, Invensys, Schneider now.
It's our illusions I recall
I really don't know us at all.

I've looked at us from both sides now
From up and down, and still somehow
It's our old history I recall
I really don't know us at all.

இ

7.3 New Sesame Street Theme Lyrics

By David Alan Hoag - October 8, 2012
(sung to the Sesame Street Theme)

Romney's way…
Taking our funds away;
Asking Bert and Ernie to compete.
Can you tell me how to fund?
How to fund our Sesame Street?

No air play…
PBS closed today;
Public TV taking all the heat.
Can you tell me how to fund?
How to fund our Sesame Street?

Romney's way…
Taking our funds away;
Asking Bert and Ernie to compete.
Can you tell me how to fund?
How to fund our Sesame Street?

❧

[Presidential debate topics sure do make for interesting political fodder. Mitt Romney got tagged as wanting to kill Big Bird! It lodged in my brain, and as so often happens, comes back out as a poem (in this case lyrics; same thing, just set to music). If you don't know the tune, crawl out from under that rock, and listen to it on YouTube.

My conservative friends will laughingly brand me a traitor, while my liberal friends will probably carry me around on their shoulders, being convinced I have finally "seen the global warming light." To everybody else, I'll just be the author of a humorous jab at politics. Enjoy.]

7.4 Did You Know Recovery's in Sight?

by David Alan Hoag - December 4, 2013
(Sung to *Santa Clause is Coming to Town*; apologies to J. Fred Coots and
Haven Gillespie)

Obama-care works,
Or so I've been told.
Jobs have returned.
This never gets old!
Did you know recovery's in sight?

He's got the right spin
Our president guy;
Republicans balk,
But why would he lie?
Did you know recovery's in sight?

Been caught domestic spying
Spied on our allies, too!
You'd better watch just what you say
'Cause he's got a file on you!

Oh…bama-care works,
Or so I've been told.
Jobs have returned.
This never gets old!
Did you know recovery's in sight?
Did you know recovery's in sight?

⌘

[Inspired by years of news headlines. It seems that whoever is in office
will generate a partisan divide as they work to somehow make good on
their political promises. Whether it was Nixon, Clinton, Bush, Obama, or
Trump… the partisan divide only seems to get wider… and more sharply
defined.]

7.5 Softball at Trabuco High

By David Alan Hoag - October 9, 2007
(Sung to *Ghost Riders in the Sky*; with apologies to Stan Jones)

A softball team went out upon a dark and windy day
The high school in Trabuco Hills the place where they would play
The Hooligans stormed toward the field, amazed the team would try
Laughing as they took the field, with a taunting smack-talk cry
Yippee aye-eh, yippee aye-ooh, softball at Trabuco High

From week to week the infamy is like a heavy stone
One wonders what the heinous sins from which they must atone
A grounder to a double play, a strikeout, or a fly
A bobbled catch, an overthrow, their gloves, too, come up dry
Yippee aye-eh, yippee aye-ooh, softball at Trabuco High

Their faces gaunt their eyes are blurred and shirts all soaked with beer
The other teams that face them know that there's no need for fear
The pitcher serves up floaters which get blasted through the sky
Soaring over fielders heads to their lone fan's anguished cry
Yippee aye-eh, yippee aye-ooh, softball at Trabuco High

The team that just seems fated to get crushed most every game
To save your soul, you'd best beware... "Triconex" is its name
And though the team will tempt you with: "you just need come and try"
Your glove will fail your bat go cold and all your skills will die
Yippee aye-eh, yippee aye-ooh, softball at Trabuco High

☙

7.6 Term! Term! Term!

Lyrics: David Alan Hoag - January 14, 2013
(Words: Adapted from The Byrds *Turn! Turn! Turn!*; music: Pete Seeger)

To everything (Term, Term, Term)
There's definition (Term, Term, Term)
And a place for explanations and new jargon

A time to propose, a time to contract
A time to plan, a time to scope
A time to code, a time to build
A time to get paid, at least we hope.

To everything (Term, Term, Term)
There's definition (Term, Term, Term)
And a place for explanations and new jargon

A time to review, a time to audit
A time to write, a time to review
A time to cast away notes, a time to gather notes together

To everything (Term, Term, Term)
There's definition (Term, Term, Term)
And a place for explanations and new jargon

A time of pro, a time of con
A time of change, a time of risk
A time you may improve, a time to refrain from improvements

To everything (Term, Term, Term)
There's definition (Term, Term, Term)
And a place for explanations and new jargon

A time to test, a time to fail
A time to stress, a time to fix bugs
A time to FAT, a time to crate
Make DE-LIVE-RY, I swear it's not too late

❧

7.7 Navy Training Chant

By David Alan Hoag - August 31, 2012

We're the Navy, we don't run;
Shipboard tanning in the sun.

We're first to sail into the fray,
To drop off troops, then sail away.

But we can fight; we get real tough,
When cooks don't serve us steak enough.

So misbehave and give us lip…
We'll toss your ass right off our ship!

Our Navy training chant's the best;
We sing this song, then need to rest.

7.8 I Get a Kick From I/O

By David Alan Hoag - October 10, 2013
(Sung to *I get a Kick Out of You*, with apologies to Cole Porter)

I get no kick from DC
Though it's *transformed*, it just has no appeal
So tell me, why should it be so
That I get a kick from I/O?

I get no kick from AC
That *alternate* leaves me flat on the *ground*
Reasons for this, I surely don't know
Yet, I get a kick from I/O.

I get a kick from raising the bar
And lifting safety so far
I get a kick that we're seen as par
We are TMR
The super star!

I get no kick from 1E
Nuclear ratings are just what we do
Our throughput's fast, where most others' are slow
Yes, I get a kick from I/O.

❧

[This song was inspired by John Gabler's illustrious past. As the story goes, John Gabler, one of the resident geniuses at Triconex, placed himself on a Safety career path as a very young child.]

7.9 Friday Friday

by David Alan Hoag - October 23, 2015
(sung to *Monday, Monday*, with apologies to John Phillips of The Mamas
and The Papas)

Friday, Friday... so good to see.
Friday, Friday... signs look like they're still payin' me.
Oh Friday mornin', Friday mornin' couldn't guarantee
That Friday evenin' Tom would still be here with me.

Friday, Friday... it's Tom's last day.
Friday, Friday... how could they let him slip away?
Oh Friday mornin' you gave me no warnin' of what was to be
Oh Friday, Friday... how could Tom leave and NOT TAKE ME?

Every other day, every other day
Every other day of the week is fine, yeah
But when any layoff comes, when any layoff comes
You can find me cryin' all of the time

Friday, Friday... so good to see.
Friday, Friday... signs look like they're still payin' me.
Oh Friday mornin', Friday mornin' couldn't guarantee
That Friday evenin' Tom would still be here with me.

Every other day, every other day
Every other day of the week is fine, yeah
But when any layoff comes, when any layoff comes
You can find me cryin' all of the time

Friday, Friday... can't trust that day
Friday, Friday... it just turns out that way
Oh Friday, Friday... Tom's goin' away
Friday, Friday... **but I must stay**!
Oh Friday, Friday
Oh Friday, Friday

[I wrote this to commemorate Tom Matheson's last day at Schneider Electric: Friday, October 30th, 2015. Tom started with Triconex, which eventually was acquired by Schneider Electric, back in 1997. He was a great engineer, a good friend, and a wonderful Christian man who lived his faith by example.]

7.10 Performer's Prayer

By David Alan Hoag - October 17, 2016

I bring to you my heart
To brighten up your day
And I hold nothing back
Each moment as I play

Let my gift break free
Loose it from all bounds
I perform awhile
Seeking to beguile
Hoping that I catch a smile

When I perform for you
On corner or in hall
I bring to you my best
I give to you my all

Let my gift break free
Loose it from all bounds
I perform awhile
Seeking to beguile
Hoping that I catch your smile

The rumble of the street
Cannot disturb my art
Nor can a cough or sneeze
Turn my performer's heart

Let my gift break free
Loose it from all bounds
I perform awhile
Seeking to beguile
Hoping that I catch your smile

Where ever I perform
I pray that I can bring
The passion and the joy
To cause your heart to sing

Let my gift break free
Loose it from all bounds
I perform awhile
Seeking to beguile
Hoping that I catch your smile

❧

[I was inspired to write this lyric after watching a video of Cal Morris beautifully playing *The Prayer* on his violin on a street corner in winter. I'd like to recognize Cal Morris for his wonderful performance, and also thank songwriters David W. Foster, Tony Renis, Carole Bayer Sager, and Alberto Testa for the original song. Additional inspiration came from my many friends who perform; whether it is in Carnegie Hall, a club, a festival, or on the street. If you play an instrument, if you juggle, mime, clown, or otherwise perform to the delight of an audience, no matter where, you have contributed inspiration to this lyric. It is written to ALL of my performer friends. If anybody has the talent, and the inclination to sing it to the melody of *The Prayer*, I'd love to hear your interpretation.]

7.11 The Island's Untold Tale

by David Alan Hoag - January 30, 1993
(with apologies to George Wyle and Sherwood Schwartz)

Well, sit right back and I'll tell the tale,
The tale of a fateful trip
That started from this tropic port
Aboard this tiny ship.

The mate was a mighty sailing' man,
The skipper brave and sure.
Five passengers set sail that day
For a three hour tour... a three hour tour.

The weather started turning rough,
The tiny ship was tossed.
If not for the courage of the fearless crew
The Minnow would be lost... the Minnow would be lost!

The ship struck ground on the shore of this
Uncharted desert isle
With Gilligan...
The skipper, too...
The millionaire... and his wife...
The movie star...
The professor and Mary Ann
Here on Gilligan's Isle.

[Now, continuing on to finish the song...]

Well, keep your seat, and I'll tell the tale,
A tale, as yet untold
Of how that group of castaways
Survived the heat and cold.

The island was inhabited
By the last of a native clan.
A scary, frightening thing he was
That Amway distributor man... that Amway distributor man!

He chased those castaways about
A wild, excited man
He wanted them to all sign up;
He said he had a plan... he said he had a plan.

But all of the shipwrecked people
Had some lame excuse
Like: "Its a cult..."
Or: "I've no time..."
And: "We don't need anything..."
"It sounds too good..."
And so, each one is stuck there still,
There on Gilligan's Isle.

❧

[This continuation of the Gilligan's Island theme song was dashed off during an Amway business conference. It poked gentle fun at our zeal to sponsor new distributors, but also was prophetic in the depiction of those that didn't want to get rescued from their rut.]

7.12 Chicken Attack

By David Alan Hoag - April 3, 2017
(Sung to *The Sounds of Silence;* apologies to Simon and Garfunkel, the Gregory Brothers, and Takeo Ischi)

Hello chicken, my old friend
I will attack with you again,
And a vision softly creeping
Started yodeling and peeping
And the vision that's been called out to attack
Has my back
Within the sound of chicken

In restless dreams I had the task
Fight a robber in a mask
He was cocky, thought I was alone
Until my chicken in the fight was thrown
And his ears were pierced by my yodels in the night
That sealed the fight
And touched the sound of chicken

And in the naked light I saw
Ten thousand chickens, maybe more
Chickens talking without clucking
Bad guys getting a good… (you know)
People yodel songs that fill the nighttime air
And no one dare
Disturb the sound of chicken
"Fools" said I
"My power has grown, in attack my chicken's flown
Hear my yodel that I might teach you
Take my chicken that it might feed you"
But my words just faded into black
On attack
Into the sky of chicken.

❧

[My friend, Clayton Sears, introduced me to the video *Chicken Attack*. Who knew yodeling was a Japanese art form? It inspired me to write my own *Chicken Attack* parody song. The original Chicken Attack video by The Gregory Brothers can be found on YouTube. Enjoy.]

7.13 The Class Theme Song

By David Alan Hoag - October 15, 1998
(Sung to *The Muppet Show Theme;* apologies to J. Henson and S. Pottle)

It's time to find our cubbies
And put our things away.
It's time to find our places
'Cause it's time to start our day.

It's time to pay attention
To hear our teacher say:
"It's time to sing this song now
'Cause it's time to start our day."

To see you all succeeding
That's what I love to do.
So it really makes me happy
To introduce to you…
The incredible…
        The remarkable…
        The awesome…
<Child's Name Here>!!!

It's time to find our cubbies
And put out things away.
It's time to find our places
'Cause we're…
        All so bright and swell…
        Uh, oh… there's the bell…
        Hey, we'd like to tell…
        That our class in swell…

This is what we call…
[Kin…der…gar…den.], or…
[The First grade class.], or… [The Second grade.], or…
[The Third grade class.], or… [The Fourth grade class.], or…
[The Fifth grade class.], or… [The Sixth grade class.]

∽

[I wrote this song for my daughter Jennifer Jerkins, the amazing teacher of young minds. Notice that it can be tailored for all elementary school grades, and to recognize individual kids by name.]

7.14 I'd Better Settle Down

by David Alan Hoag - July 11, 2019
(Sung to *Ghost Riders in the Sky*)
(with apologies to Stan Jones)

A restless boy who'd gone to bed
Just couldn't settle down.
He tossed and turned both back and forth
Which made his mother frown,
For she was in the next room
And could hear his bunk bed pound.
Its squeaking and its shaking noise
Did echo all around.

The darkened room was suddenly
Thrown into garish light.
His mama flung the door aside,
Her figure quite a sight.
A bolt of fear went through him as
He hunkered down in place,
He saw the anger in her eyes
And that look upon her face.

Oh, Mom is mad
And I've dis-tur-urbed her,
I'd better settle down.

What's going on, what have we here?
Why aren't you sleeping, boys?
What's causing all this shaking?
And what is that squeaking noise?
You'd better settle down right now
And get yourselves to sleep.
The shaking and the squeaks must stop,
Now, not another peep!

Oh, Mom is mad
And I've dis-tur-urbed her,
I'd better settle down.

As Mother left and shut the door
The boys were cowed and sad,
They hadn't thought their rattle-ings
Would make their mother mad.
So children, when you go to sleep
Best settle down in place,
For otherwise you're doomed to see
Your mother's angry face!

Oh, Mom is mad
And I've dis-tur-urbed her,
I'd better settle down.
I'd better settle down.
I'd better settle...
I'd better settle down.

[My grandsons, Jeffrey Delgado and Bob Jerkins, to one's mortification and the other's delight, were the inspiration for this fun song, with its origins in actual events.]

7.15 The Sound of Sniffles

By Marie Martin and David Alan Hoag - December 27, 2010
(Sung to *The Sound of Silence*, with apologies to Paul Simon)

Pseudoephedrine, my old friend... I've come to ask your help again.
Because a head cold slowly creeping
Would get worse while I am sleeping
And the blockage that keeps oxygen from my brain
Still remains
With the sound of sniffles.

In restless dreams I sneeze alone
Call the ER on the phone
Sit alone in their full waiting room
There with my sinus pounding out my doom
When my eyes were stabbed by the flash of a TV screen
A drug I'd seen
To stop the sound of sniffles

And in the TV's light I saw
Ten thousand people, maybe more
People talking without sneezing
People hearing without sniffling
People living lives that sniffles never touch
Oh, please, how much...
To buy the drug for sniffles?

"Fools", said I, "You do not know
Dependence on the drug will grow
Hear my words that I might teach you
Take my arms that I might reach you"
But my words, like silent raindrops fell
And echoed
In the wells of sniffles

And the people bought the spray
To cure the fever from the hay
And the bottle had a warning
That you might be dead by morning
And the drug said, "The words of the warning are written in a font most fine
And found online
Still you'll buy it to cure... your sniffles

[Marie Martin, in writing the first verse of this song and posting it on Facebook, became my muse for this particular night! After reading her post, I was moved to complete the song, title it, and (finally) credit the original songwriters.]

7.16 B. I. C. – Boyz In Confirmation

by David Alan Hoag - May 15, 1999
(Sung to a rap beat)

We're the Boyz!
We're the Boyz!
We're the Boyz in the Confirmation clan
And we walk with God 'cause He has a plan.

Matt, C. J., Kyle… to name a few,
Justus, Ian, Michael… rounding out the crew.

We're the Boyz!
We're the Boyz!
We're the Boyz in the Confirmation clan
And we walk with God 'cause He has a plan.

God's had a plan since He first made the light,
But humanity sins, and we can't get it right.
He gave us commandments and taught us to pray,
But we keep messin' up, and continue to stray!

Well, I've got questions, and issues, and stuff.
I try to do my best, but it's never enough!
If my nature is sin… in frustration I cry:
If I always mess up, why then should I try?

God knew that only His own sacrifice
Was the sole offering that would ever suffice!
So he came as a babe, not a king, or the boss,
But we all ran away… let him die on a cross.

Yet He rose, and he promised… His Spirit is near.
When we walk in His light, there is nothing to fear.
No prison will hold us… not wire, nor bars,
'Cause He paid our release, now Heaven is ours!

We're the Boyz!
We're the Boyz!
We're the Boyz in the Confirmation clan
And we walk with God 'cause He has a plan.

You MAY see a boy, but I'm becoming a man!
Which is why I'm here, to scope out God's plan.
So I can be what he wants me to be,
And learn to live in God's family.

We're the Boyz!
We're the Boyz!
We're the Boyz in the Confirmation clan
And we walk with God 'cause He has a plan.

We fear the Lord, but we don't walk in fear,
'Cause we walk with God. See… our Savior is here!

We're the Boyz!
We're the Boyz!
We're the Boyz!
We're the Boyz!

✍

[Back in 1999, I was a Confirmation Guide at a Lutheran church. I wrote this song as a fun performance piece for the boys in my class. The boys practiced, and wanted to perform for the congregation some Sunday. The pastor was willing, but all of us adults forgot we were dealing with 13-year old boys. What they claimed to be able to do, and what they could actually accomplish were worlds apart. When it came to the actual performance, they pretty much froze up. As you might imagine, the world tour opportunity, recording deal, and merchandizing deals did not materialize. Perhaps YOU are the rapper with the talent to perform this song. Good luck!]

7.17 The Sounds of Safety

By David Alan Hoag - May 03, 2007
(Sung to *The Sound of Silence*, with apologies to Paul Simon)

Hello darkness, my old friend
They've changed our logo once again.
The color that they tell us now is gray,
Is still a black percentage anyway,
And the safety vision planted in our brains
Still remains;
We call ourselves… Triconex.

Though you might search both near and far
We are the only TMR,
And though the others all may claim to be,
Alone, we're certified through TUV
And readers who were polled in Control Magazine
Their choice was seen
The last ten years… Triconex.

And in each safety case I saw
Ten million hours, maybe more.
Plants depending on their safety state
Continue running without pause or wait,
And the issues that were causing shutdown wear
Were just not there
We're TMR… Triconex.

The experts say you'd be a fool
If your system's only dual
Hear my words: "Don't trust your field device,
Alone, its safety data won't suffice,
Yet the safety data's there for the blind to see."
It echoes in the halls… of Triconex.

And plant managers, they prayed
To the DCS they made.
Yet their plant could blow without warning
From the safety faults it was forming,
And the sign said: "The words of plant safety are at TUV
For all to see,
And whispered in the name... Triconex."

7.18 It's Scott and Dan

It's Scott And Dan

By David Alan Hoag - December 27, 2017
(Sung to "Anything Goes" with apologies to Cole Porter)

It used to be, a magic lecture
Would bore you with dull conjecture
But, man-oh-man,
It's Scott and Dan.

Two guys that are not stiff and haughty
And well known for being naughty
A show-biz ban,
It's Scott and Dan.

If smashing up phones you like,
If neck bones you like,
If froggies you like,
If cookies you like,
If it's Puck you like,
Or a f _ _ _ you like,
Well then, find it here you can.
When shopping for some magic, that is new
You find dec'ades of Déjà vu
In a snake can
It's Scott and Dan.

When playing Jeopardy with magical
Big stars that now are tragical
And dumber than
Both Scott and Dan.

A milk and cookies trick, quite snappy;
Hiding a ring in bubble wrappy,
No better than
Scott and Dan.

They plugged the Tarbell today,
Update hell today,
DVDs today,
Killing sprees today,
Karnak spoof today,
Makeup goof today
Made them look pale and wan.
And though their shows are fun and tasty
But as they are white and pasty,
They need a tan.
It's Scott and Dan.

As lectures go, this one was funny,
Really more than worth the money.
I'm a big fan
Of Scott and Dan!

❧

[Scott Alexander and Dan Harlan of Penguin Magic host a yearly Christmas show that is part show, part lecture, and all irreverent. I love the creative peek behind the curtain of a bunch of strange and magical minds. This was my review, in song.]

7.19 I'm Off to Take a Journey

By David Alan Hoag - September 8, 2010
(Sung to *We're Off to See he Wizard*, with apologies to E. Y. Harburg and Harold Arlen)

Fly in my hot-air balloon. Fly in my hot-air balloon.
Flying, flying, flying, flying...
Fly in my hot-air balloon.
Fly in my hot-air balloon. Fly in my hot-air balloon.
Fly in my hot-air balloon.

I'm off to take a journey, A journey that takes me from Oz.
Hazardous is, this trip for your Wiz! If ever a trip there was.
It's technically unexplainable 'cause, the stratosphere mostly makes your head buzz,
Because, because, because, because, because.
Because it's what atmosphere always does.
I'll soon confer with wizards... Your hobnobbing Wizard of Oz.

[Bree Rhoten posted a creative challenge on Facebook: "What does the Wizard sing when he is off to see someone?" I could not resist coming up with this song, a parody of *We're Off to See the Wizard (Follow the Yellow Brick Road)*.]

7.20 Dust in the Bag

by David Alan Hoag - September 25, 2019
(Sung to the Kansas song "Dust in the Wind"; apologies to Kerry Livgren
and Kansas)

I check my list, got the salsa, now I need a bag of chips.
I scan the aisle, all the bags look perfect, but it's just a dream.
Chips in the bag
Dreaming of whole chips in the bag.

Then at home, I tear into the bag and wonder what I see
All the chips, are crushed to dust. How could this have come to be?
Dust in the bag
All the chips are dust in the bag.

Oh, oh, oh… [instrumental bridge]

It's just a dream, all the bags look perfect when they're in the store
But chips get crushed, nothing much can save them once they're out the door.
Dust in the bag
All the chips are dust in the bag.
[(Echo:) All the chips are dust in the bag.]
Dust in the bag
[(Echo:) All you get is dust in the bag.]
All you get is dust in the bag.

❧

[Inspiration, as you probably guessed was simply opening a bag of chips
and finding… nothing but tiny bits of crushed chips.]

8 ODES

An ode is a lyric poem praising or glorifying an event or individual, describing nature intellectually as well as emotionally.

We have the ancient Greeks to thank for creating this type of lyrical stanza. A classic ode is structured in three major parts: the strophe, the antistrophe, and the epode. Different forms such as the homostrophic ode and the irregular ode also exist.

My odes reflect my personality, and thus could only be categorized as the irregular type.

8.1 Ode to the PM's Delivery

by David Alan Hoag - October 23, 2014

You guide, you lead… to no avail;
It's so much more than herding cats.
Oh, look! There's the transmittal trail!
And so I offer you Con-Gratz!

✄

[This was just a quick email response to Project Manager as he posted notification of an important project delivery/transmittal to one of our customers. We're talking a LOT of paperwork… generated, reviewed, and verified by teams from V&V, Quality, and Delivery. It's an ode because I titled it as such.]

8.2 Growing Up Too Fast

by David Alan Hoag - August 17, 2015

Seems like only yesterday
That for you to get some rest,
I'd sit in the big rocker,
And you'd sleep upon my chest.

You'd hardly talk, yet you made
For each animal its sound.
To read, you would command us:
"Sit," and pat the chair or ground.

Your "eeep-eeep" changed to "monkey",
Though I'm not sure why or how,
Followed by another change,
When your "moo-moo" became cow.

Since seven, you've been reading
An amazing little wiz
It's not seven years I mean,
Seven months of age, that is!

Tickle/wrestling in the bed;
Something that you loved to do
Made special on that morning,
To hear: "Pop-pop, I love you!

[Inspired by my granddaughter, Emma Portillo; almost 22 months of age, as of this writing.]

8.3 Extinction

by David Alan Hoag - April 19, 2013

Dragons roamed in ancient times;
A senseless, random power.
None could predict their rampage;
Not day, and not the hour.

Wreathed in smoke and bathed in flame,
With a seething, senseless mind
A dragon wrecks destruction
Of extremely violent kind.

So it was... until the world,
On dragons placed a bounty.
Thus, it was, brave men arose
From village, town, and county.

Many died, in fervent haste
To rid the land of wyrms.
Spurred to heroic action
By the bounty's generous terms.

At first, there was confusion
There were snakes, and crocs, and such...
But bounties paid on dragons,
Weren't collected overmuch.

Dragons are known as loners
Thus, not easy to gestate
But men breed unrestricted;
Tend to over-populate.

In growing zeal to slay them,
Men stacked corpses up in piles
Few ever found a dragon,
So... fear for the crocodiles!

[I wrote this during the manhunt for those responsible for the Boston Marathon bombings in April, 2013. In many ways, the dragon metaphor turned out to be well suited to the unfolding story.]

8.4 Ode ad Draconis Infinitas

by David Alan Hoag - October 30, 2013

We doze, though not within the realm of what you sense,
For you inhabit but the world between;
A tiny spectrum of a vaster whole,
From atoms to vast galaxies, unseen.

Hibernation, that's the wrong measure that you'd use
Describing us within time's ebbs and flows;
Unmoving, not alive, to you it seems.
Our kind, we never fully sleep... we doze.

And though we're generally aware of all you do,
We've naught to add, and even less to prove.
While mindful of your need to be restrained,
Inertia makes it very hard to move.

Now bound within a cooling, iron-nickel sphere
We dream the dreams of dragons; so sublime:
To soar magnetic flux and plasma streams,
To overcome the bounds of space and time.

Your kind must see and touch. YOUR senses make it real?
In stories, tales, and myths of every kind
Do you not think it strange to see us there?
Ah, dragons... out of sight, thus out of mind.

Up thrusts occur when we would lay our bodies down
Inert for millennia, as we chose
Our Dragon's teeth, our Dragon's back, our tail;
Erosion will oft parts of us expose.

Look! Your cities quake, when we shudder in our doze
And when we wake, you'd best know dragon lore.
Mountains will crumble, seas will rise and fall.
Pray we doze a few millennia more.

&

8.5 Yana Reznik's Lost Performance

by David Alan Hoag - May 3, 2013

A microphone might capture notes
In digital perfection.
So also, with a camera lens,
But just in one direction.

When cameras work, and mics record,
They can catch performing, whole.
All that aside, they still can't catch
Yana's bright and brilliant soul.

Lost power to the battery,
Or a broken circuit board;
For whatever glitchy reason,
The device did not record.

It's more than just the music's sound,
And it's more than just the sight.
There's a very real connection
On a live performance night.

She can move a hall to silence,
Or a great, collective sigh,
Or free them from their mundane world,
As they close their eyes and fly.

Her fingers dance, caress the keys,
In acrobatic fashion,
And no device can catch, or hold
Her power, or her passion.

✤

[Yana Reznik's problem recording a performance inspired this poem. Besides being incredibly talented, stunningly beautiful, and full of life, energy, and joy… Yana is a creative Muse to many, especially her many artistic friends.]

8.6 Satisfying the Ghost

by David Alan Hoag - October 29, 2013

So strangely scored, with eerie sound
Haunting, called The Ghost
Written with Marie in mind, to
Thank a gracious host.

The Master's Opus Seventy
For a trio scored
Reznik, on piano shone, as
To new heights they soared.

With Lisker and Lifschitz on strings
As they played they found
Their talents lifted everyone
To a perfect sound.

How well Artistic Voyage played
Everyone was moved.
The ghost, Ludwig, at last revealed
Silently approved.

✦

[The Artistic Voyage Trio of... David Lisker, Yana Reznik, and Eugene Lifschitzplaying Ludwig van Beethoven's Ghost Trio opus 70 inspired this poem.

http://www.youtube.com/watch?v=mVztGDtE4wM&feature=youtu.be

If you can find it on YouTube (try the link, above), you can watch the Artistic Voyage Trio perform.]

8.7 Ever Changing Profile

by David Alan Hoag - October 12, 2013

She turns her head and gazes out
Oh, what has caught her eye?
A sunset sparkle on a wave,
Or something in the sky?

There is a joy that most outgrow
Left in our childish youth:
The beauty that's in everything;
A glorious, hidden truth.

What we already overlooked
Has caught her questing sight
And when we look again, we find,
We bask in her delight!

Some call her "Angel"; others, "Muse";
What more could heaven send?
I know she stirs a joy in me...
I'm blessed to call her friend.

Yana Resnik is a friend of amazing talents who changes her profile picture quite a bit. That may only be noteworthy to lumbering dinosaurs of my generation who haven't changed their profile picture since the last century, but her mercurial changes often inspire my imagination. Sometimes, the inspiration will bubble over into some form of poetic expression... this was one of those creative moments.

8.8 On a Creative Note

by David Alan Hoag - June 17, 2019

A beautiful image
An image in blue
An image that captures
The essence of you.

The world pulls you hither
And yon, every day
Both forwards and backwards
Quite every which way.

Though everything round you
May stretch and may change
You never will limit
Your destiny's range.

Your vision is piercing,
But, so too your gaze
It touches our soul, sets
Our vision ablaze.

You invite us to share
Your passion, your joy
By the uncommon way
Your love you employ.

So when we're around you
We're desperate to use
Each fast ticking second
While blessed by a Muse.

We, left in LA, feel
An empty, cold pain
Though Cali lost Yana,
It's Chicago's gain.

❧

[Yana Resnik posted this picture to her Facebook page in 2014 as she was about to embark on a move from Los Angeles to Chicago. I wanted to write a poem, but I was too busy with work, grandkids, and lack of sleep. At that time, I only managed to post a note on her Facebook page, as follows:

"Beautiful, beautiful, beautiful! I keep coming back to this image that captures you so well. The world might pull you in multiple directions, but you are rock-solid. Everything around you may stretch, may change, may be distorted, but you never waiver from your vision or your destiny. Most amazing, though, is that piercing gaze of yours that reaches into our very souls... inviting us to share your vision of creative passion, love, and joy. We are blessed to share moments with you. For myself, I'm awed that I should know a Muse! Chicago is in for a BIG surprise... called Yana!"

FIVE YEARS LATER: I finally bumped into the note again. This time, the intersection of time and creative energy produced the *On a Creative Note* poem, above.]

8.9 Love One Another

by David Alan Hoag - June 30, 2019

There's something quite special
When you are first met
You change people's lives, but
They don't know it yet.

You're gracious and gen'rous
We know in the end
It only gets better
When you call us friend

New friends become family
Wherever they roam
Just moments with you, and
They feel right at home

Your children are whip-smart
And talented, too
Great character traits that
They picked up from you

At church, work, or ballfield
You stand apart
While most seem standoffish
You lead with your heart

And when, if our orbits
To deviate start
Reunions feel like we
Were never apart

You bless all with something
They're unaware of
As instinctive as breathing
You mirror Christ's love.

[This is an ode to my good friends, Matt and Loree Bowen. From the moment people first meet them, they recognize they've encountered something special. Folks want to be around Matt and Loree. They have 4 amazingly intelligent, generous, and talented kids... which speaks volumes to the awesome character of their parents.]

8.10 Joaquin's

by David Alan Hoag - July 1, 2019

Out on the old Yorba Ranch
In a plaza. Off to the side
Is a little Cantina
That's known for its food far and wide

Megan serves drinks at the bar
Margaritas, served up with style.
No doubt, the liquor's a draw,
But people return for her smile.

Order a Mexican drink
They'll serve you a bottle of beer
Double X or Corona
They call it cerveza, I hear.

Joaquin's is up on the sign.
Décor is eclectic and wild.
They serve chips with hot salsa;
For Gringos, they'll serve up the mild.

Jesus and Marcos hold court
They're servers who always have been
Working hard for us patrons,
And owners, that's Gary and Lynn.

"Just what will you order to eat?"
A tough little question to solve,
So come back week after week…
And let a tradition evolve.

༚

[The food, employees, and the owners make Joaquin's restaurant really amazing. We've frequented Joaquin's for more than 30 years, so it must truly be special!]

9 CHRISTMAS CARDS

In 2014, aiming to combat boring Christmas newsletters, I blurred the lines between the reality people experience and the dramatic fiction they often feel to be overwhelming them around the Holidays. *Sharing Christmas* (published by Xlibris) is my collection of original Christmas-themed writings, Christmas songs, Christmas cards, and Christmas-themed poetry that took form over the years.

The book is about Christmas, but that subject encompasses everything from the commercial to the holy, the historic to the hysterical, and the presents humans give, to the presence of God they can receive. I started out with simple notes that I enclosed in commercial Christmas cards to my closest friends. Eventually, it evolved over the years into self-designed cards, which became very popular. The cards were printed in such a way that produces a Christmas card after two successive folds of the paper. There was usually a picture or graphic on the front accompanied by one of my original songs or poems in the middle with a blessing.

In today's society, Christmas is rapidly being perceived as a commercial or retail buying and selling season. Now, more than ever, the world needs to hear the message of love, peace, joy, forgiveness, and salvation... that is the real message of Christmas.

I'm unapologetic in stating that I believe that *Sharing Christmas* perfectly captures the spirit of the Yuletide Season through my original poetry, songs, and cards. It was a true labor of love.

Sharing Christmas
By David Alan Hoag
Hardcover | 8.5x8.5in | 58 pages | ISBN 9781503514584
Softcover | 8.5x8.5in | 58 pages | ISBN 9781503514591
E-Book | 58 pages | ISBN 9781503514607
Available at Xlibris, Amazon, Barnes & Noble, and most booksellers

Sharing Christmas included Christmas writings and Christmas cards from 1997 through 2014. This section contains original Christmas card material from 2015 through 2019.

9.1 2015 Christmas Card - A Savior Has Been Born to You

by David Alan Hoag - December 09, 2015

While prepping for Christmas,
We've been quite torn apart
By murderous shooters
With a dark, hate-filled heart.

For humanity's soul,
Terror's not a new thing;
Was used that first Christmas
By Herod, the king.

Each one of us matters!
Shepherd's heard angel's call:
"So do not be afraid,
I bring good news for all."

It's still true to this day:
For you REALLY to know,
Like those shepherds of old,
You must get up, and go.

Shepherds had to proclaim
What they'd seen, what they'd heard.
When your joy overflows,
You can't help spread the word

God sent Jesus to Earth,
Us salvation to give;
Not just freedom from sin,
But the best way to live.

Merry Christmas to You!
This Christmas, the words of Psalm 51:10 bring hope:
"Restore to me the JOY of your salvation..."

**May this Christmas season bring you love, peace, and uncontainable joy
to fill your heart, and your New Year, too!**

9.2 2016 Christmas Card - Welcome to the Family

by David Alan Hoag - December 8, 2016

Here's a Christmas card to contemplate
Meant to challenge what we know.
Why is Christmas set in wintertime?
Do we need the Christmas snow?

While in another hemisphere
Christmas sleigh bells never ring
No chestnuts, and there's no snowmen
While their summer's in full swing.

The babe wasn't born a Christian,
He was born a baby Jew,
And Joseph and his wife, Mary?
Turns out they were Jewish, too.

A tree, with lights, and ornaments
Wasn't there, which gives me pause.
And truth be told, there was no sign
Of all-knowing Santa Claus.

Inviting ALL, angels revealed
It's not who or what you know;
The Magi sought the baby out,
With the lowest of the low.

A baby doesn't take a test,
It belongs on its first day.
It doesn't need to learn some Creed,
Or profess ALL that they say.

Christmas… reminds that followers
Of Christ Jesus, from the start…
Belong. Then grow. Then learn to serve.
As God's love… fills up their heart.

❧

Merry Christmas to You!

This season, let the words of Psalm 37:4 guide you through Christmas, and into the New Year:

"Delight yourself in the LORD and he will give you the desires of your heart."

9.3 2017 Christmas Card - Angels Rejoiced

by David Alan Hoag - December 10, 2017

While the angels rejoiced
At the birth of the child
Singing of peace on earth
And of us reconciled.

While the peace from above
Humbly came to the earth,
A new age was dawning
With the infant child's birth.

God knows we need saving
For we won't change our ways
And for wages of sin
It's true, EVERYONE pays.

Yet, with the babe's coming
We could turn a new page
But something was missing
For, still we kill and rage.

Men tried to contain it
Sealed it up in a grave
But Good News… it broke free
That salvation God gave.

How can it be contained
In a day, or season,
This grace of God, His Son,
Our joy beyond reason?

Well, it can't be contained
So perhaps Christmas day
You'll follow a new path
Jesus called it "The Way."

Merry Christmas to You!

This Christmas, I pray that you get past the trappings of the season to discover and embrace the gift that God has given to all of us.
Unwrap God's gift to you… it's the best present ever!

9.4 2018 Christmas Card - A Christmas Message

by David Alan Hoag - December 18, 1979

Only the children,
And young ones at that,
Believe in the man
With the red suit, who's fat.

But now you can know
In your heart that I'm real,
And not just a figment
Of some merchant's zeal.

For down from the pole
I come, yearly, unswerving,
To make an appearance
To those quite deserving.

And what should I see
From my sleigh as I flew?
But the fact that there's
No one deserving like you!

For, your normal habit
Of sharing and giving,
Keeps Christmas a season
That's vibrant and living.

So stay glad of heart,
And spread Christmas all year.
…From the man with the beard
…And eight tiny reindeer.

⤏

[Back in 1979, the people I worked with all chipped in to buy our secretary a much-needed watch. It was placed in her car where she could find it, along with this poem. Is there someone who needs YOUR compassionate help, some encouragement, or just a kind word this Christmas season?]

Merry Christmas to You!

9.5 2019 Christmas Card – A Christmas Wish

By David Alan Hoag - October 15, 2019
(Sung to *A Whole New World*, from Aladdin; apologies to Alan Menken and Tim Rice)

You can have a new life
Loving, joyful; with purpose
You can exit the circus
And leave that old life behind.

There's a light in this world
Calling you to a new start
Reimagining your part
In a life to be reborn.

A Christmas wish
A non-commercial holiday
No need to shop in malls
Or deck the halls
Or wear an ugly sweater

A Christmas wish
A season greeting you can say
Welcome the Christ Child in
And die to sin
For God has come to birth a brand new day

Just let go of the weight
All your sins, so unsavory
Jesus frees you from slavery
To pursue a brand new life.

A Christmas wish
It's not a decorated tree
It's like the light of day
Chased fears away
The world is made brand new for you and me.

A Christmas wish
A wish that never will be done
A wish that when unfurled
Is for the world
God has sent this wish to everyone

A Christmas wish
How can this be?
A baby's birth
Brings peace on earth
For you and me

❦

This season, I pray that you see past the commercial spectacle that the world touts as Christmas, and discover the promise of a life embracing the message of Jesus.

I love sharing Christmas with you! Merry Christmas!

10 GEOCACHING RELATED

Geocaching is a real-world, outdoor treasure hunting game using GPS-enabled devices. Participants navigate to a specific set of GPS coordinates and then attempt to find the geocache (usually a container of some sort) hidden at that location.

My geocaching username is Cigam Mai. The name has a deeper meaning that is easy to discern, even for the most backward. Like David often shortens down to Dave, Cigam Mai was often just Cigam or Cig. The following geocaches, with their associated poems, were created and maintained by me.

10.1 Cigam Finds The Da Vinci Codes - Part 1

by David Alan Hoag – August 13, 2004

With Fibonacci you will find the key
That will reveal a secret unto thee
Sum to EACH portion of the geo-flow
Ascending sequence values as they go

❧

[Geo-flow:
N (2)(2) (3)(-3).(4)(-4)(-9)
W (-20)(-33)(-48) (-42).(584)

This was written for a mystery cache called *Cigam Finds The Davinci Codes (Archive waypoint: GCK8WM)*. Inspired by Dan Brown's book, *The Da Vinci Code*, the poem portion was published backward, so you'd have to use a mirror to read it correctly. It was originally published in a flowery script font to add an additional layer of confusion to the puzzle. You needed to decipher the poem to even figure out where to start.

The cache has long since been disabled, but if you are a puzzle solver you can put your little gray cells to work to solve the multiple puzzles of this geocache. Everything you need to get started is provided in the poem above. The "geo-flow", when computed correctly would yield the GPS coordinates of what would turn out to be the next step of a rather diabolical puzzle.

The solution may be found in Chapter 12.

10.2 Cigam Finds The Da Vinci Codes - Part 2

by David Alan Hoag – August 13, 2004

Once you decrypted the first clue, the coordinates would lead you to eventually discover a camouflaged tin hidden in the leaf-choked crook of a mature eucalyptus tree. Inside the tin were identical slips of paper that contained a clue for the next step of this multi-stage puzzle.

The clue strip looked like this:

The Clue:

Line Grade Tooth = The Golden Ratio

5421587.928 hip biddy dive

7260632.880098887515451174289246 time ship

iph sequal eno pinot xis noe thige

[You were instructed on the inside of the tin to take a clue slip, so that you could re-hide the tin for the next geocacher. Clue in hand, you were free to find a comfortable location where you could decrypt this next puzzle. Can you figure out what the clue means without consulting the solution?

The solution may be found in Chapter 12.]

10.3 Cigam Finds The Da Vinci Codes - Part 3

by David Alan Hoag – August 13, 2004

Once you figured out the clue to Part 2, the decrypted coordinates would lead you to eventually discover a camouflaged tin hidden in the center of a rotting tree stump in the middle of a dense thicket (think Whomping Willow). Inside the tin were identical slips of paper that contained the clue for the next step of this multi-stage puzzle. In this case, the initial, and very obvious, clue was a poem I wrote in iambic pentameter.

The Clue:

> Encryption codes not quite your cup of tea?
> Well, then, I'll toss a clue in here for free.
> A simple substitution code… it seems.
> why, then, the anguished moans and muffled screams?

---

rivs rava rreug gavbc rava lgebs qan arrgarirf qreqahu rab gfrj, fqabprf ehbs lgkvf qreqahu bjg qan frghavz lgsvs frretrq rreug lgevug ugeba

---

					N						
					A						

[You were instructed on the inside of the tin to take a clue slip, so that you could re-hide the tin for the next geocacher. Clue in hand, you were free to find a comfortable location where you could puzzle out this next puzzle. Can you figure out what the clue means without consulting the solution?

The solution may be found in Chapter 12.]

10.4 Cigam Finds The Da Vinci Codes - Part 4

by David Alan Hoag – August 13, 2004

Once you solved Part 3, the decrypted coordinates would lead you to eventually discover the final grail cup containing the geocaching log and associated treasures.

Hidden in plain sight, this final cache container could be surprisingly difficult to find. The Cache page describes it as follows:

> *The final grail cup is but a simple 1 ¾-inch diameter by 2 ½-inches deep container (bring small stuff to trade). The cup itself is hidden in something that displays astonishing obedience to the Devine proportion.*

Truly, this was a Cache was a secret… guarded by a puzzle… wrapped in a conundrum.

[Even when you had done everything correctly, finding the final container was a challenge, both mentally and physically. See Chapter 12 for a description of the container, and how it could be located.]

10.5 Cigam Casts a Hex

by David Alan Hoag - October 12, 20??

A puzzle meant to tease and vex
How base of me to cast a Hex
Text encoded, but what's the key?
An offset shift... what can that B?
Oh... one more rule you must abide,
The code is 26 a side!
So don't use digits... they're pristine.
To code them, too, would just be mean.

❧

[Cigam's Hex:

C 33 51 03.40 L 117 47 38.76 LXAA IPZT NDJ ID P RAJQ, QJI IWT
WTM IWPI WPH UGDOTC IWT VXGPUUTH XH PI CDGIW
IWXGIN IWGTT STVGTTH UXUIN DCT BXCJITH PCS OTGD
UDJG EDXCI ILTCIN UDJG HTRDCSH LTHI DCT WJCSGTS
HTKTCITTC STVGTTH UDGIN HTKTC BXCJITH PCS UXUIN
EDXCI HXMIN HTKTC HTRDCSH.

I really enjoyed putting this puzzle together, but this cache was never activated. Geocaching rules only allow one cache within any tenth of a mile radius. I was too slow posting, and another cache beat me into the area. If you solve it, you can still discover the magic this cache solution leads you to.

The solution may be found in Chapter 12.]

10.6 Cigam Rides Again

by David Alan Hoag - July 6, 2003

I stand alone; connected though
To all my brothers, to and fro.

We stand to make the equine race
More apt to follow bit and trace.

You want a clue... I'm sensing that
From underneath my peaked, white hat.

Make me tip my hat to you;
The only way... silver to view.

Lift the silver from its lair,
To find my red cap lurking there.

Give my red cap but a twist,
Then add your name onto the list.

Now just reverse what you have done,
Perpetuating caching fun.

∽

This was written for a cache called Cigam Rides Again. The poem gives several clues about the location of the cache. The posted coordinates took you right to the correct location. The cache container was hidden inside a fence post along a horse trail. Once found, all the clues in the poem make sense.

10.7 A Bird in the Hand

Once again... the cache container has been stolen!

Sigh... the mental processes of this persistent container thief (or more likely, lack thereof) are definitely beyond my understanding. I'm guessing that whomever it is that persists in purloining the cache containers is probably simian... in nature, physical attributes, and mental acumen. I seriously hope they get professional help, or at least a banana. More likely, due to the timing of stolen containers, the thief is probably on some sort of 60-day work/release program from the local prison, or mental asylum.

Whew... that was cathartic! Seriously, though, if you are the thief, if you are reading this, and if you can prove that you are the thief... I will supply you at regular intervals with BETTER swag than what you are currently stealing, if you just STOP taking the cache containers. Oh, and for good measure, I'll even throw in a container each time... since you seem to love old peanut butter jars so much.

There once was a Muggle, who'd brag:
"A birdie supplies me with swag.
　　　There's a log, and toy car,
　　　And it comes in a jar,
Complete with a 'Don't Take Me' tag!"

❧

Sigh... actually, the thief, other than taking the containers, has caused no damage to the construction itself. Many cachers break things when they don't read the instructions, or when they use brute force (when NONE is required). So, in a way, I guess the thief is relatively harmless.

REMEMBER... this is a BAD PLACE to leave Travel Bugs... as they are LIKELY to be stolen!

11 RuneScape Related

My RuneScape username was Cigam Mai. In games like RuneScape or World of Warcraft, you play by controlling an avatar across the various domains of the game worlds. You are known only by the name you give to your avatar. My avatar's name had a deeper meaning that was easy to discern, even for the most backward (hint, hint). Like David often shortens down to Dave, Cigam Mai was often just Cigam or Cig.

I was recruited into a RuneScape clan called The Sith Order (TSO). It had rules, structure, and some awesome leaders, but it also had its share of immaturity, infighting, and upheavals over time. I stayed loyal and committed to the Sith Order while I was active in RuneScape.

I served TSO in many official capacities, which may seem strange to those unfamiliar with virtual game play. Our commitments weren't just to the avatars on a video screen, but to real-life, flesh and blood people who could connect across oceans and continents in a virtual space, in ways not possible in the real world. Friendships cultivated in the virtual worlds of RuneScape live on in Facebook and real world connections. For a few players, I've been delighted to watch them mature, earn degrees, embark upon careers, get married, have children, and stay in touch… even though most of us have never met face-to-face.

The virtual environment of RuneScape could be a wonderfully inspiring place. I soon became known as the Bard of TSO. I have no idea just how much poetry I created in RuneScape, as most of it was on the fly. I did manage to save some bits and pieces over the years, but many a poem was lost to the moment. What follows are bits of poetry that are all related to RuneScape, and especially my time in TSO. Though they comprise several different poetic genres, they all have the fabric of RuneScape woven into their DNA. You may find RuneScape poems in other sections of this book.

Like RuneScape, my poetry in this section can be epic, fun, silly, or thought-provoking. As you read on, I hope you discover a sense of adventure amongst the silliness and fun. Good luck!

11.1 Party Hat

by David Alan Hoag - April 29, 2012

Ah, you're young, and might be in a phase;
Perhaps confused, maybe in a haze.
I see what you are doing, really pays.
Wish "I" had a billion... nice hat, Daze!

∽

[My friend, and TSO clan mate, Daze Eclipse, had just purchased a party hat... for 1 billion gold coins! Party hats were basically just a hat; no special powers or protection were granted to the wearer. Their enormous price tag was because they were so incredibly rare. I was in awe, and to tell the truth... inspired. If Daze wanted anything more elegant than the doggerel poem I'd written, he would need to commission it.

Just in case anyone was in the market for the kind of immortality that only a bard could provide, I decided to post my pricing:

Free Verse: 100,000 gold coins
Simple Rhyme: 500,000 gold coins
Haiku: 2 million gold coins
Limerick: 5 million gold coins
Iambic Pentameter: 10 million gold coins
Sonnet: 50 million gold coins
Epic Poem: 500 million gold coins

Each poem would include their name, of course. Their great deeds, battle prowess, and awesomeness would also be included… as the structure and meter of the various poetic forms would allow. Obviously, the cheaper poems were offers for the noobish masses. Only the most elite of RuneScape players would see the value of commissioning an epic poem to ensure that their greatness would be properly immortalized. Surprise, surprise... nobody took advantage of the deal.]

11.2 The Sith Order

By Cigam Mai - May 10th, 2010

I'll tell you a tale of a fantastic place
That is filled with the beings of many a race.
It is only through questing, battles, and travel
That some of the strangeness begins to unravel.
But the very best day for the virtual man
Is the day he's accepted in TSO's clan.

Though RuneScape, in itself, is a virtual land
Its adherents make up a fanatical band
Of denizens logged on… both by day and by night
Either busily crafting, or picking some fight,
Or ambushing players… some weaker, some stronger;
Don't say addicted. But they keep playing longer!

While playing a mini, Berzerk showed me a plan
Of how I should apply, and join TSO's clan.
The Sith Order clan, as he explained it to me
Was just the right place for a plus-ninety to be.
I logged into the clan chat; found quite the uproar,
But was helped out and welcomed by Gimila4.

Gim, as I called him, was on a lot, to be frank,
You could count on him always to update a rank.
Newbies (I was one) would ask: "What is T. S. O.?"
He'd answer their question; let no frustration show.
"And F. T. W.?" they would ask with a grin :)
Then Gim always replied: "It just means: 'For The Win.'"

Gim goaded me once to slay brine rats for training
It's where I met Morg; a new friend I was gaining.
And in the wee hours, with just Gim, Morg, and I
We'd train, laugh, and encourage… as hours flew by
I would often bring Darth… like us, quite crazy, too,
Who would round out the humor, and add to our crew.

There was always some drama, some nose out of whack
Some people would leave, but then we'd welcome them back.
Too often the fights touched both the great and the small,
But I never thought fights could so impact us all.
A struggle for power… I'd oft seen it before,
But when the dust settled, I found Gim was no more!

From his TSO family, he was sent packing
Now his teaching and wit will sorely be lacking.
I'm not placing the blame (though there's plenty for all)
But there's no place for 'that' type of fame in our Hall.
"Offer forgiveness!" that, I have been appealing.
Forgiveness must come first; then follows the healing.

With so much experience, and ninety-nine ranks
Gim helped me a lot. For that, I offer my thanks.
And should my excitement get poor, or start waning
Gim pushed me along, my Attack he was training.
But much sweeter, by far, than a cape for Attack
Was the swelling excitement that: "Gimila's back!"

To be Sith is a promise that no one can kill.
For a time we were dead and death did drink its fill,
And those snakes who attacked with their guile and their lies
Were surprised, from the ashes, to see us arise
By Lord Gimila's actions, he helped us to learn…
Though the Sith may seem dead, they will always return.

Our Sith commitment can't be bought; it can't be owned.
Embracing the Dark, the Sith thrive… but can't be cloned.
Though lost souls may claim our length, our breadth, or our width,
There is no impostor that can equal the Sith.
From the Galaxy's core to its frontier and border
The Dark Side is the realm of the awesome Sith Order.

❧

[This poem was my tribute to The Sith Order, and many of its memorable members.]

11.3 Wishing for Relief

By David Alan Hoag - July 16, 2012

I wish I was an octopus,
With tentacles and suckers.
I'd wrap them 'round annoying bots,
And crush those cheating… Noobs.

✎

[This poem was written as a surprise; in frustration at the large number of bots (automated players; annoying AND illegal) that were swarming RuneScape at the time.]

11.4 Cannonballs

By Cigam Mai - September 10, 2010

Cannonballs are pricey,
Or so the story goes…
I just find they hurt me,
when dropped upon my toes.

[Just an answer to someone complaining about the cost of… you guessed it… cannonballs.

It was necessary to stick to short poems, like this, in order to stay current in the conversation stream within the game.]

11.5 Dragons

By Cigam Mai - September 10, 2010

Remember friends, when fighting Dragons…
Always be at your fighting best…
Best not to laugh your ass off…
Or the beast will fry the rest!

[I wrote this after witnessing a player get killed by a dragon. It was totally avoidable, and only happened because the player wasn't paying attention to the game. Instead, the player was trash-talking and laughing at a fairly new player. The resultant death was pretty funny, ironic, and fodder for the creation of this poem.]

11.6 Terah

By Cigam Mai - September 17, 2010

Terah is right, Terah speaks true
More likely than not, Terah's speaking to you.
So shape up; no rudeness… don't fight.
You don't want to feel all her Chancellor's might!

∾

[A poem I dashed off as a friendly warning to TSO clan members in RuneScape. Terah Blair was Chancellor of the TSO clan at that time. She was fun, fair, level-headed, and an accomplished and powerful player within the RuneScape gaming environment.]

11.7 Member Bonus

by Cigam Mai - May 02, 2012

Old Jagex, with their crafty ways
Made May a month that truly pays,
Determined not to be outdone
June is also looking fun.

[As usual, it paid to be a member!]

11.8 Of Cabbages and Kings

by Cigam Mai - November 01, 2010

The Emperor, Blake, and Terah
Were walking close at hand
The beach was wide
From side to side
But much too full of sand

"Mr. Cigam," said the Chancellor
"My brain begins to perk
We'll do a Sweep in just a week
If you don't mind the work"

"Work?!? The time has come," old Cigam said
"To talk of other things
Of shoes and ships and sealing wax
Of cabbages and kings
And why the sea is boiling hot
And whether pigs have wings
Calloo-Callay
Sweep starts today!
Of cabbages and kings"

&

[Member sweeps were common occurrences among clans. You added your name to a list you copied into a clan post (bump the Thread). It was a way to verify that players active in the clan. It was time for another sweep and Lewis Carroll provided most of the inspiration for this poem. Due to the great preponderance of youthful players, and the steadfast refusal of most of them to explore much literature outside of their gameplay, nobody got the reference to either the Walrus, the Carpenter, or their conversation in *Through the Looking Glass*. Truth be told, the Walrus and the Carpenter song from the Disney animated version of *Alice in Wonderland* is what was actually rattling around in my head.]

11.9 Drawn

by Cigam Mai - January 23, 2011

A wave upon the shore
Cresting far out to sea
What's doing all the pulling?
What's the force we cannot see?

They say tidal forces
Shift oceans constantly
Can the moon exert such force?
Is it really gravity?

A man upon the shore
Questing far out to sea
What's doing all the pulling?
What's the force we cannot see?

What pulls him onward so?
To what end be his goal?
Why explore and ever seek?
What's the force that pulls his soul?

Restless indeed is he
And seeks to sail and fly
In all creation only
He is always asking "Why?"!

❧

[While engaged in repetitive training within the RuneScape universe (farming, fishing, combat training, etc.) player conversations could range from the banal to the philosophical, from the wickedly funny to the wickedly ribald, and everything in between. A young player called Pen, who was actually a teen living in the United Arab Emeritus, surprised us one night with a very introspective bit of questioning prose. His questions were the catalyst for the poem, above.]

11.10 MCM Entry

by Cigam Mai - May 10, 2012

I should get two tickets to MCM because...

I'm TSO's famed Cigam Mai...
I should win, since I am magic...
In verse, I give you my reply...
MCM sans me, is tragic!

∽

[The Movie Comic Media (MCM) Expo Group was the organizer of the London Comic Con, and Jagex (the maker of RuneScape) was running a ticket challenge for tickets to the London Comic Con MCM Expo. I thought the clan might enjoy my entry (above), and that it might inspire some of them to come up with their own brilliant answer to:

"I should get two tickets to MCM because..."

It did not.]

11.11 Lumbridge

by Cigam Mai - July 27, 2013
(sung to Don McLean's *Vincent)*

Lumbridge lies in ruin
Now become a battleground
Screaming with the silent sound
Of gods that join in battle once again

Smoke upon the hills
Overflow of battling wills
Source of all our human ills
In tears upon the desolated land

Now, I understand, what Guthix tried to say to me
And how he suffered for humanity
And how he tried to set us free
We would not listen, we did not know how
Perhaps we'll listen now

Flaming, flaming day
Fiery shards that brightly blaze
Swirling clouds of emerald haze
Reflect in clashing beams of red and blue

Striving of the gods
Battlefields of human pain
All because one god would reign
What matter that they win a ravaged land?

Now, I understand, what Guthix tried to say to me
And how he suffered for humanity
And how he tried to set us free
We would not listen, we did not know how
Perhaps we'll listen now

For they could not love you
But still your love was true
And when no hope was left inside
On that fateful, fateful night
You gave yourself; the only thing to do
But I could have told you, Guthix
This world was never meant to live
As balanced as you do

Flaming, flaming day
Altars built for gods most high
Reckless gods who'd have us die
To tip their scales in ways they can't, as yet

Like the warriors that you've met
Though mighty sword and gleaming shield
Though valor on the battlefield
Lie crushed and broken on the plane of death

Now, I think I know
What Guthix tried to say to me
And how he suffered for humanity
And how he tried to set us free
We would not listen, we're not listening still
Perhaps we never will.

∾

[This song makes a lot more sense if you know the gods of the RuneScape universe. Guthix is a god of balance.]

11.12 King Black Dragon

by David Alan Hoag (Cigam Mai) - November 25, 2013
(Sung to Puff, the Magic Dragon)

Oh, old King Black Dragon, in his cavern lair
Would battle teams, from warrior clans, in battles not quite fair.
Oft the Sith would hear, a call to battle ring,
Then travel through the Wilderness to fight that Dragon King. Oh...

Old King Black Dragon, in his cavern lair
Would battle teams, from warrior clans, in battles not quite fair.
Old King Black Dragon, in his cavern lair
Would battle teams, from warrior clans, in battles not quite fair.

Together we would travel through dangerous Wildy lands
Sith leaders kept a lookout for marauding player bands.
Other noble players would often follow suit
And join with us in battle, and share in all the loot. Oh...

Old King Black Dragon, in his cavern lair
Would battle teams, from warrior clans, in battles not quite fair.
Old King Black Dragon, in his cavern lair
Would battle teams, from warrior clans, in battles not quite fair.

A dragon spawns forever, so also do the Sith
Often, though, reality just doesn't fit the myth.
One update it happened, and the Sith clan came no more
And that mighty Dragon King, he ceased his fearless roar.

The Sith and Jedi balance; one more, the other less.
Sith no longer march in file, along the Wilderness.
Most Sith now wander Old School, among the fierce and brave,
And that old Black Dragon King, lies lonely in his cave. Oh...

Old King Black Dragon, in his cavern lair
Would battle teams, from warrior clans, in battles not quite fair.
Old King Black Dragon, in his cavern lair
Would battle teams, from warrior clans, in battles not quite fair.

11.13 They Spawn Anew Each Wednesday Morn

by David Alan Hoag (Cigam Mai) - December 15, 2010
(sung to: It Came Upon a Midnight Clear; apologies to Edmund Sears)

They spawn anew each Wednesday morn,
Those sneaky penguins from the cold.
They hide in bushes, crates, and rocks
To help their plans unfold.
They hide themselves to spy on us
You know they are up to no good;
In frozen wastes, they plan and scheme
Our overthrow, if they could.

Just how they manage to plant their spies;
A mystery we haven't unfurled,
But still they send them to spy on us
O'er all the Runescape world.
Throughout the deserts, or Wildy flames,
Their camo makes them hard to see
And though we trap them as best we can
More oft than not they run free.

Yet with his ignorance, greed, and strife,
The penguins' ultimate plan,
Is far beneath the notice of
The ceaseless striving of man;
And man, at war with man, hears not
Their camouflage clockworks that tick;
O hush the noise, ye men of strife
And hear the penguins click.

And ye, beneath life's crushing load,
Whose forms are bending low,
Who toil along the climbing way
Ye seek high levels, but slow.
Look now! For glad and golden hours
Come swiftly on penguins' wing.
O rest beside the weary road,
And hear the penguins sing!

For lo! the days are hastening on,
By Fremmenik-bards foretold,
When with the ever circling years
Comes round the age of gold;
When peace shall over all the earth
Its ancient splendors fling,
And the whole world send back the song
Which only penguins sing.

❧

[This was my penguin Christmas song. Penguin hunting was a RuneScape activity that could help players level their stats quickly, and in a fun way. There was a forum thread called "Penguin Locations", which was a MUST READ for the serious penguin hunter in RuneScape!]

11.14 My Avatar Gently Weeps

by Cigam Mai - October 2, 2011
(sung to George Harrison's *While My Guitar Gently Weeps*)

I look at this world
See the talent that's sleeping
While avatars gently weep
And in a few hearts
There's a darkness that's creeping
Still avatars gently weep

You don't know why you can't be loyal
It just unfolds that way
If you would learn you could be royal
Open a bright new day

And some in each clan
Are continually grumbling
While avatars gently weep
In many a Keep
There are walls that are crumbling
Still avatars gently weep

Don't know why you anger at slighting
Was it all you were taught?
You may get rich from all that fighting
But wisdom can't be bought

I look at this world
See the talent that's sleeping
While avatars gently weep
In a few hearts…
My avatar gently wee-ee-eeps.

෯

[Inspired by clan events during RuneScape gameplay.]

12 PUZZLE SOLUTIONS

Here are the puzzle solutions. Only the solutions are shown on this page, so you can check your work. It's easy for mistakes to creep in, so if you find your solution still a bit off, you can go back, check your assumptions and calculations, or return to the drawing board entirely.

Flummoxed? At your wits end? Are you ready to throw in the towel? Well then, just turn to the corresponding subsection and you will find a complete explanation along with the answer.

Here are JUST the solutions:

1. The Davinci Code - Part 1
   N 33 50.944, W 117 47.728
   Complete explanation in Section 12.1
2. The Davinci Code - Part 2
   N33° 50.796 W117° 47.704
   Complete explanation in Section 12.2
3. The Davinci Code - Part 3
   N33° 50.264 W117° 49.395
   Complete explanation in Section 12.3
4. The Davinci Code - Part 4
   Pinecone Cache Container
   Complete explanation in Section 12.4
5. Cigam Casts a Hex
   N 33 51' 04.24", W 117 47' 50.67"
   Complete explanation in Section 12.5

12.1 Explanation: Cigam Finds The Da Vinci Codes - Part 1

With Fibonacci you will find the key
That will reveal a secret unto thee
Sum to EACH portion of the geo-flow
Ascending sequence values as they go

⸎

Geo-flow:
N (2)(2) (3)(-3).(4)(-4)(-9)
W (-20)(-33)(-48) (-42).(584)

Explanation:
The poem provides several clues:
1. "Fibonacci" is virtually synonymous with the Fibonacci Sequence
2. The poem says to "sum" the ascending sequence to "EACH portion of the "geo-flow"; so, add the obvious GPS coordinates to the ascending values of the Fibonacci sequence.

The Fibonacci values are easily computed, but if you are not a mathematician, the first 12 values of the Fibonacci sequence are:

1,1,2,3,5,8,13,21,34,55,89,144

Thus, summing the two sequences results in:

N 1+2=3; 1+2=3; 2+3=5; 3-3=0; 5+4=9; 8-4=4; 13-9=4
W 21-20=1; 34-33=1; 55-48=7; 89-42=47; 144+584=728

Final GPS coordinates led to a camouflaged cookie tin hidden in the leaf-cluttered fork of a eucalyptus tree. The correct coordinates work out as:

N 33 50.944, W 117 47.728

If you had read Dan Brown's *The Da Vinci Code*, all of this would be pretty obvious, if not... dust off that math degree.

12.2 Explanation: Cigam Finds The Da Vinci Codes - Part 2

The clue strip should have revealed itself to be an obvious set of anagrams.

The Clue:

Line Grade Tooth = The Golden Ratio

5421587.928 hip biddy dive

7260632.88009888751545117 4289246 time ship

iph sequal eno pinot xis noe thige

The Anagram Puzzle Solution, in 5 parts:

1. Part 1
   a. Clues within clues.
   b. "Line Grade Tooth" is an anagram of "The Golden Ratio", therefore they are equal.
2. Part 2
   a. Solving the remaining anagrams.
   b. hip biddy dive - divided by phi
   c. time ship - times phi
   d. iph sequal eno pinot xis noe thige - phi = 1.618
3. Part 3
   a. Understanding phi.
   b. Phi = Golden Ratio = The Devine Proportion = 1.618
   c. "Spiraled pinecone petals, sunflower seed spirals, leaf arrangement on plant stalks, insect segmentation… all displaying obedience to the Devine Proportion." – The Da Vinci Code
4. Part 4
   a. Solving the calculations.
      i. 5421587.928 divided by phi = 5421587.928/1.618 = 3350796
      ii. With proper notation, it becomes: N33° 50.796
      iii. 7260632.88009888751545145174289246 times phi
      iv. = 7260632.88009888751545145174289246*1.618 = 11747704
      v. With proper notation, it becomes: W117° 47.704
5. Part 5
   a. Assembling the final coordinates leading to the next piece of the puzzle.
   b. N33° 50.796 W117° 47.704

12.3 Explanation: Cigam Finds The Da Vinci Codes - Part 3

This clue strip immediately shows itself to be a substitution code.

The Clue:

Encryption codes not quite your cup of tea?
Well, then, I'll toss a clue in here for free.
A simple substitution code... it seems.
why, then, the anguished moans and muffled screams?

---

rivs rava rreug gavbc rava lgebs qan arrgarirf qreqahu rab gfrj, fqabprf
ehbs lgkvf qreqahu bjg qan frghavz lgsvs frretrq rreug lgevug ugeba

---

					N						
					A						

The Substitution Code Solution, in 4 parts:

1. Part 1
   a. Fill in the decryption table from the given clue.

H	I	J	K	L	M	N	O	P	Q	R	S	T
U	V	W	X	Y	Z	A	B	C	D	E	F	G

2. Part 2
   a. Translate the message using the substitution code decryption table. It doesn't initially make much sense, as it now reads:
   b. "evif enin eerht tniop enin ytrof dna neetneves derdnuh eno tsew, sdnoces ruof ytxis derdnuh owt dna setunim ytfif seerged eerht ytriht htron"

3. Part 3
   a. Viewed backwards (like Da Vinci's notes) the message now reveals:
   b. "North thirty three degrees fifty minutes and two hundred sixty four seconds, West one hundred seventeen and forty nine point three nine five."

4. Part 4
   a. Therefore, the numerical representation of the coordinates that lead to the final piece of the puzzle are:
   b. N33° 50.264 W117° 49.395

12.4 Explanation: Cigam Finds The Da Vinci Codes - Part 4

Once you solved Part 3, the decrypted coordinates would lead you to eventually discover the final grail cup containing the geocaching log and associated treasures.

Hidden in plain sight, this final cache container could be surprisingly difficult to find. The Cache page describes it as follows:

> *The final grail cup is but a simple 1 ¾-inch diameter by 2 ½-inches deep container (bring small stuff to trade). The cup itself is hidden in something that displays astonishing obedience to the Devine proportion.*

Truly, this was a Cache was a secret… guarded by a puzzle… wrapped in a conundrum.

The Final Secrets Revealed:

The coordinates decrypted from the clue of Part 3 lead to a different park in Anaheim Hills, California from where the first parts of this puzzle began.

If you entered the park and parked in its parking lot, you had a steep uphill climb to the Cache coordinates. The area around the coordinates was part of a wild canyon slope, covered in pines, manzanita, and scrub; tough going from the well-maintained park at the floor of the canyon. At the top rim of the canyon, however, was a business park. It had plenty of parking, and was only an easy downhill walk to a little-used trail leading from the top of the canyon down into the park, AND easy access to the final coordinates.

Once at the final coordinates, you found yourself in the midst of a small stand of pine trees and plenty of underbrush, and you still had to find the container; described as being about the size of a tin can. Indeed, that's exactly what the cache container was... a tin can! Of course, to make it harder to find, I had epoxied pinecone petals around the can until it looked exactly like the dozens of other pinecones in the area. Its cover and hook were attached securely to the can, so that its camouflage fell right into place when it was hooked to a branch of the pine tree.

Teams of geocachers managed to solve the entire mystery, with all of its puzzles, in a surprisingly short amount of time. The cache only lasted about a year, as heavy rains destabilized the area around the final cache location. Several pine trees fell over, including the one with the pinecone container hung from its branches. The area was marked by the park service as dangerous, and off limits. When the trees fell, the container was damaged. Rather than start over, I decided to just archive the whole thing. It had a good run, and nothing lasts forever.

12.5 Explanation: Cigam Casts a Hex

A puzzle meant to tease and vex
How base of me to cast a Hex
Text encoded, but what's the key?
An offset shift... what can that B?
Oh... one more rule you must abide,
The code is 26 a side!
So don't use digits... they're pristine.
To code them, too, would just be mean.

I wrote this for a puzzle cache. The poem is the key to an offset code. The offset is B... in Hex (hexadecimal number base)... so in decimal, the offset is 11. All other characters (including numbers are not coded. So, by shifting the alphabet offset by 11, the code key then becomes:

Code	a	b	c	d	e	f	g	h	i	j	k	l	m
Alphabet	l	m	n	o	p	q	r	s	t	u	v	w	x
Code	n	o	p	q	r	s	t	u	v	w	x	y	z
Alphabet	y	z	a	b	c	d	e	f	g	h	i	j	k

With the key, the following message...

C 33 51 03.40 L 117 47 38.76 lxaa ipzt ndj id p rajq, qji iwt wtm iwpi wph ugdotc iwt vxgpuuth xh pi cdgiw iwxgin iwgtt stvgtth uxuin dct bxcjith pcs otgd udjg edxci iltcin udjg htrdcsh lthi dct wjcsgts htktcittc stvgtth udgin htktc bxcjith pcs uxuin edxci hxmin htktc htrdcsh.

decrypts to...

N 33 51 03.40 W 117 47 38.76 will take you to a club, but the hex that has frozen the giraffes is at north thirty three degrees fifty one minutes and zero four point twenty four seconds west one hundred seventeen degrees forty seven minutes and fifty point sixty seven seconds.

N 33 51' 04.24", W 117 47' 50.67"

The "club" of the decrypted message is the Auto Club office in Anaheim Hills, which has safe and ample parking. From the Auto Club parking lot, it's less than a 350-meter walk to the coordinates that will reveal the giraffes that have supposedly been frozen by a hex. They are, of course, sculptures of giraffes; surprising to see in somebody's backyard!

13 FINAL THOUGHTS

Is there something that you really loved about this book? I'd enjoy having you send me an e-mail describing what you liked, and why. Corrections and other editorial comments will also be given due consideration. Of course, I have a very strong kinship with a character in Lewis Carroll's *Through the Looking-Glass*, who said:

"When I use a word," Humpty Dumpty said in rather a scornful tone, "it means just what I choose it to mean - neither more nor less."

Final Thoughts

by David Alan Hoag - September 1, 2019

You've come to the end
Did you read the whole thing?
Or maybe just read one or two?
If your final thoughts
On this book are all good
Perhaps you could write a review.

Contact me at: **ybic.dave@rith.biz**
Check out my blog at: **http://aliveinthespirit.blogspot.com/**

INDEX OF POEMS

2015 Christmas Card 193

2016 Christmas Card 194

2017 Christmas Card 196

2018 Christmas Card 198

2019 Christmas Card 200

A Bird in the Hand 210

Accidental Causes 41

Adam's Birthday..63

A Father's Questions 91

Aim High..12

Alexander, Scott..173

A Limerick for Gary Wilkinson 70

A Limerick for Mark Lehman 73

A Limerick for Omed Muzaffrey..74

A Line for Dad's Seventieth.. 114

American Life: Power 112

Barker, Allen..76

Basis of Fact 32

Beans? Again?..83

Be My Valentine..117

Blair, Terah..3, 219

Both Sides Now..146

Bowen, Loree 189

Bowen, Matt 189

Boyz In Confirmation..168

Bridge Support 5

———

245

Brush Strokes 104

Cannonballs 217

Can You Hear Me Now? 10

Chicken Attack 160

Cigam Casts a Hex 208

Cigam Finds The Da Vinci Codes - Part 1 204

Cigam Finds The Da Vinci Codes - Part 2 205

Cigam Finds The Da Vinci Codes - Part 3 206

Cigam Finds The Da Vinci Codes - Part 4 207

Cigam Rides Again 209

Circadian Rhythm Sanity Check for Couples 13

Citizen Soldier 94

Close Shave 4

Communicator 14

Communicator Colors 15

Creative Yanamation 6

Currency of the Dead 77

Delgado, Jeffrey 86, 93, 165

Did You Know Recovery's in Sight? 149

Diversity 62

Doc Martin's B-Day 31

Door Repair Request 21

Dragons 218

Drawn 222

Dust in the Bag 175

Eternity 140

Eulogy 128

Ever Changing Profile 185

Explanation: Cigam Casts a Hex 240

Explanation: Cigam Finds The Da Vinci Codes - Part 1 232

Explanation: Cigam Finds The Da Vinci Codes - Part 2 234

Explanation: Cigam Finds The Da Vinci Codes - Part 3 236

Explanation: Cigam Finds The Da Vinci Codes - Part 4 238

Extinction 180

Failure Modes and Effects Analysis 84

FBC Pickers 78

Final Thoughts 243

Finger on the Pulse 121

Fitness for Duty 22
For Allen Barker 76
Forgiving Heart..36
For Glory...58
Fourth of July 57
Friday Friday 154
Gabler, John 153
Get with the Program 24
Glimmering Hope..56
Glitter and Glue..106
Gorm Grymme 38
Greg Eyvazian's Lament 28
Growing Up Too Fast 179
Hard Rock Valentine...108
Harlan, Dan 173
Harris, Steve..82
Hernandez, Cassandra 16
Hernandez, Catarina..16
Hoag, Barbara 134
Hoag, Ian 95
Hoag, Lillian...131
Hoag, Michael...125
Hoag, Patti .... xiii, 64, 106
Houlbrook, Nick 66
Hufton, Gary 68
I Am So Frozen..145
I'd Better Settle Down 164
If Only...30
I Get a Kick From I/O..153
I'm Off to Take a Journey...174
In Honor of Monica Martin's Cat Returning Home 25
In the Hurricane's Wake 90
It Seemed So Easy..102
It's Scott and Dan..172
Jerkins, Bob 93, 165
Jerkins, Henry 93
Jerkins, Jennifer 64, 65, 91, 93, 163
Joaquin's 190

King Black Dragon 226
Knocking...100
Krausman, Michael 30, 86
Lake Forest Apiary..122
Lanier, Paul Francis 100
Lappa, David..67
Larson, Jeffrey 126, 127
Legacy 20
Lehman, Mark 73
Lifschitz, Eugene 184
Limerick for David Lappa..67
Limerick Power 85
Love One Another 188
Lumbridge...224
Lunar Dreams 88
Magic 99
Management 101...2
Martin, Diehl...92
Martin, Marie 31, 166
Martin, Monica...78
Matheson, Tom 155
MCM Entry..223
Me Grandma..130
Member Bonus..220
Meza, Velinda 9, 14
Michael Hoag - In Memoriam 124
Morris, Cal..157
Muscovy Duck 80
Muzaffery, Omed..74
My Avatar Gently Weeps...230
Naus, Carol 23
Navy Training Chant 152
New Sesame Street Theme Lyrics 148
Nick's Birthday...66
Ode ad Draconis Infinitas...182
Ode to the PM's Delivery 178
Of Cabbages and Kings 221
Omed Moved 75

On a Creative Note 186

On My Mother's Passing...134

On Vacation 61

Palmer, Janice 80

Party Hat...213

Penguin Magic 173

Performer's Prayer 156

Phoenix Rises 132

Pirate's Lament...34

Portillo, Adam 63

Portillo, Emma...179

Portillo, Wendy 64, 65

Read and Sign 68

Requiem 141

Reznik, Yana 6, 10, 18, 53, 183, 184, 185, 187

Rhoten, Bree 174

Romney, Mitt...148

Santa Ana Winds..116

Satisfying the Ghost..184

Scales, Miranda..5

Scalia, Barbara 69

Scalia, Joe 69

Scouting The Territory..69

Sears, Clayton 161

Seeley, Brad 56

Send-off...93

Shower Challenge 64

SNAFU...72

Softball at Trabuco High..150

Softball Game Tonight 35

Stopping by Triconex on a Rainy Evening 115

St. Paddy's Day with Velinda 9

Stuntman...86

Terah 219

Terah's Finals 3

Term! Term! Term! 151

Thanksgiving Reflections 98

The Art of a Muse 44

The Class Theme Song 162
The Clueless Father of Daughters 96
The Crossing 136
The Island's Untold Tale 158
The Real Diehl 92
The Reminder 127
The Sith Order 214
The Sound of Sniffles 166
The Sounds of Safety 170
The Trench 16
They Spawn Anew Each Wednesday Morn 228
Ties That Binder 26
Time 17
Time Dilation Task 8
Time Off 82
To My Lover 107
Treasure 65
Triconex 35, 68, 76, 115, 146, 150, 153, 155, 170
True Quality 126
Twister 81
Unfit Bit 23
Unseen Power 111
Waterman, Dave 80
Waving Goodbye 138
What Prize? 79
Wilkinson, Gary 70
William and Kate 110
Wishing for Relief 216
With a Whimper 129
Witnessed by Clowns 118
Yana Reznik's Lost Performance 183
Yana's Road Not Taken 18
Yoda's Take on Proposals 29

CPSIA information can be obtained
at www.ICGtesting.com
Printed in the USA
BVHW031035271219
567959BV00005B/82/P

9 781796 069921